10/19
958.1 Nel

GENOCIDE & PERSECUTION

I Afghanistan

Titles in the Genocide and Persecution Series

GENOCIDE & PERSECUTION

I Afghanistan

David E. Nelson
Book Editor

Frank Chalk
Consulting Editor

GREENHAVEN PRESS
A part of Gale, Cengage Learning

GALE
CENGAGE Learning·

Detroit • New York • San Francisco • New Haven, Conn • Waterville, Maine • London

Elizabeth Des Chenes, *Director, Publishing Solutions*

© 2013 Greenhaven Press, a part of Gale, Cengage Learning

Gale and Greenhaven Press are registered trademarks used herein under license.

For more information, contact:
Greenhaven Press
27500 Drake Rd.
Farmington Hills, MI 48331-3535
Or you can visit our Internet site at gale.cengage.com.

For product information and technology assistance, contact us at:

Gale Customer Support, 1-800-877-4253
For permission to use material from this text or product, submit all requests online at www.cengage.com/permissions

Further permissions questions can be emailed to permissionrequest@cengage.com

Every effort is made to ensure that Greenhaven Press accurately reflects the original intent of the authors. Every effort has been made to trace the owners of copyrighted material.

Cover Image Credit: © Bettman/Corbis.
Interior barbed wire artwork © f9photos, used under license from Shutterstock.com.

LIBRARY OF CONGRESS CATALOGING-IN-PUBLICATION DATA

Afghanistan / David E. Nelson, book editor.
    pages cm. -- (Genocide and persecution)
    Includes bibliographical references and index.
    ISBN 978-0-7377-6251-8 (hardcover)
1. Afghanistan--History--Soviet occupation, 1979-1989. 2. Afghanistan--History--1989-2001. 3. Afghanistan--History--2001- 4. Political violence--Afghanistan. 5. Crimes against humanity--Afghanistan. 6. Human rights--Afghanistan. 7. Afghan War, 2001- 8. Taliban. 9. Afghanistan--Politics and government--20th century. I. Nelson, David E., compiler.
    DS371.2.A33815 2013
    958.104--dc23

                                                            2012049971

Printed in the United States of America
1 2 3 4 5 6 7 17 16 15 14 13

Contents

   Patricia Gossman

   A human rights consultant provides a concise history of human rights
   abuses and war crimes in Afghanistan since 1978.

   Boris Gromov

   In an internal document sent to Soviet ambassadors following Afghanistan's April 1978 Communist revolution, the Central Committee of
   the Communist Party of the Soviet Union blames the post-revolution
   political strife and violence on external pressure from the United States,
   Pakistan, and China.

   The Democratic Republic of Afghanistan

   The Soviet-controlled Afghan government indignantly responds to
   President Jimmy Carter's January 23, 1980, State of the Union address,
   in which Carter characterizes the Soviet presence in Afghanistan as
   an attempt "to subjugate the fiercely independent and deeply religious
   people of Afghanistan."

   Felix Ermacora

The United Nations reports on Soviet atrocities committed in Afghanistan such as unlawful imprisonment, torture, the targeting of civilians, and the conscription of child soldiers.

Chapter 2: Issues and Controversies Surrounding Afghanistan

A foreign affairs advisor argues that Soviet forces used chemical weapons against both Afghan insurgents and civilians, which was a violation of international law.

Chapter 3: Personal Narratives

Preface

> *"For the dead and the living, we must
> bear witness."*
>
> *Elie Wiesel, Nobel laureate and
> Holocaust survivor*

The histories of many nations are shaped by horrific events involving torture, violent repression, and systematic mass killings. The inhumanity of such events is difficult to comprehend, yet understanding why such events take place, what impact they have on society, and how they may be prevented in the future is vitally important. The Genocide and Persecution series provides readers with anthologies of previously published materials on acts of genocide, crimes against humanity, and other instances of extreme persecution, with an emphasis on events taking place in the twentieth and twenty-first centuries. The series offers essential historical background on these significant events in modern world history, presents the issues and controversies surrounding the events, and provides first-person narratives from people whose lives were altered by the events. By providing primary sources, as well as analysis of crucial issues, these volumes help develop critical-thinking skills and support global connections. In addition, the series directly addresses curriculum standards focused on informational text and literary nonfiction and explicitly promotes literacy in history and social studies.

Each Genocide and Persecution volume focuses on genocide, crimes against humanity, or severe persecution. Material from a variety of primary and secondary sources presents a multinational perspective on the event. Articles are carefully edited and introduced to provide context for readers. The series includes volumes on significant and widely studied events like the Holocaust, as well as events that are less often studied, such as the East Pakistan genocide in what is now Bangladesh. Some volumes focus on multiple events endured by a specific people, such as the Kurds, or multiple events enacted over time by a particular oppressor or in a particular location, such as the People's Republic of China.

Each volume is organized into three chapters. The first chapter provides readers with general background information and uses primary sources such as testimony from tribunals or international courts, documents or speeches from world leaders, and legislative text. The second chapter presents multinational perspectives on issues and controversies and addresses current implications or long-lasting effects of the event. Viewpoints explore such topics as root causes; outside interventions, if any; the impact on the targeted group and the region; and the contentious issues that arose in the aftermath. The third chapter presents first-person narratives from affected people, including survivors, family members of victims, perpetrators, officials, aid workers, and other witnesses.

In addition, numerous features are included in each volume of Genocide and Persecution:

- An annotated **table of contents** provides a brief summary of each essay in the volume.
- A **foreword** gives important background information on the recognition, definition, and study of genocide in recent history and examines current efforts focused on the prevention of future atrocities.
- A **chronology** offers important dates leading up to, during, and following the event.
- **Primary sources**—including historical newspaper accounts, testimony, and personal narratives—are among the varied selections in the anthology.
- **Illustrations**—including a world map, photographs, charts, graphs, statistics, and tables—are closely tied

to the text and chosen to help readers understand key points or concepts.

- **Sidebars**—including biographies of key figures and overviews of earlier or related historical events—offer additional content.
- **Pedagogical features**—including analytical exercises, writing prompts, and group activities—introduce each chapter and help reinforce the material. These features promote proficiency in writing, speaking, and listening skills and literacy in history and social studies.
- A **glossary** defines key terms, as needed.
- An annotated list of international **organizations to contact** presents sources of additional information on the volume topic.
- A **list of primary source documents** provides an annotated list of reports, treaties, resolutions, and judicial decisions related to the volume topic.
- A **for further research** section offers a bibliography of books, periodical articles, and Internet sources and an annotated section of other items such as films and websites.
- A comprehensive subject **index** provides access to key people, places, events, and subjects cited in the text.

The Genocide and Persecution series illuminates atrocities that cannot and should not be forgotten. By delving deeply into these events from a variety of perspectives, students and other readers are provided with the information they need to think critically about the past and its implications for the future.

Foreword

The term *genocide* often appears in news stories and other literature. It is not widely known, however, that the core meaning of the term comes from a legal definition, and the concept became part of international criminal law only in 1951 when the United Nations Convention on the Prevention and Punishment of the Crime of Genocide came into force. The word *genocide* appeared in print for the first time in 1944 when Raphael Lemkin, a Polish Jewish refugee from Adolf Hitler's World War II invasion of Eastern Europe, invented the term and explored its meaning in his pioneering book *Axis Rule in Occupied Europe.*

Humanity's Recognition of Genocide and Persecution

Lemkin understood that throughout the history of the human race there have always been leaders who thought they could solve their problems not only through victory in war, but also by destroying entire national, ethnic, racial, or religious groups. Such annihilations of entire groups, in Lemkin's view, deprive the world of the very cultural diversity and richness in languages, traditions, values, and practices that distinguish the human race from all other life on earth. Genocide is not only unjust, it threatens the very existence and progress of human civilization, in Lemkin's eyes.

Looking to the past, Lemkin understood that the prevailing coarseness and brutality of earlier human societies and the lower value placed on human life obscured the existence of genocide. Sacrifice and exploitation, as well as torture and public execution, had been common at different times in history. Looking toward a more humane future, Lemkin asserted the need to punish—and when possible prevent—a crime for which there had been no name until he invented it.

Legal Definitions of Genocide

On December 9, 1948, the United Nations adopted its Convention on the Prevention and Punishment of the Crime of Genocide (UNGC). Under Article II, genocide

> means any of the following acts committed with intent to destroy, in whole or in part, a national, ethnical, racial or religious group, as such:
>
> (a) Killing members of the group;
> (b) Causing serious bodily or mental harm to members of the group;
> (c) Deliberately inflicting on the group conditions of life calculated to bring about its physical destruction in whole or in part;
> (d) Imposing measures intended to prevent births within the group;
> (e) Forcibly transferring children of the group to another group.

Article III of the convention defines the elements of the crime of genocide, making punishable:

> (a) Genocide;
> (b) Conspiracy to commit genocide;
> (c) Direct and public incitement to commit genocide;
> (d) Attempt to commit genocide;
> (e) Complicity in genocide.

After intense debate, the architects of the convention excluded acts committed with intent to destroy social, political, and economic groups from the definition of genocide. Thus, attempts to destroy whole social classes—the physically and mentally challenged, and homosexuals, for example—are not acts of genocide under the terms of the UNGC. These groups achieved a belated but very significant measure of protection under international criminal law in the Rome Statute of the International Criminal

Court, adopted at a conference on July 17, 1998, and entered into force on July 1, 2002.

The Rome Statute defined a crime against humanity in the following way:

> any of the following acts when committed as part of a widespread and systematic attack directed against any civilian population:
>
> (a) Murder;
>
> (b) Extermination;
>
> (c) Enslavement;
>
> (d) Deportation or forcible transfer of population;
>
> (e) Imprisonment or other severe deprivation of physical liberty in violation of fundamental rules of international law;
>
> (f) Torture;
>
> (g) Rape, sexual slavery, enforced prostitution, forced pregnancy, enforced sterilization, or any other form of sexual violence of comparable gravity;
>
> (h) Persecution against any identifiable group or collectivity on political, racial, national, ethnic, cultural, religious, gender . . . or other grounds that are universally recognized as impermissible under international law, in connection with any act referred to in this paragraph or any crime within the jurisdiction of this Court;
>
> (i) Enforced disappearance of persons;
>
> (j) The crime of apartheid;
>
> (k) Other inhumane acts of a similar character intentionally causing great suffering, or serious injury to body or to mental or physical health.

Although genocide is often ranked as "the crime of crimes," in practice prosecutors find it much easier to convict perpetrators of crimes against humanity rather than genocide under domestic laws. However, while Article I of the UNGC declares that countries adhering to the UNGC recognize genocide as "a crime under international law which they undertake to prevent and to punish," the Rome Statute provides no comparable international mechanism for the prosecution of crimes against humanity. A treaty would help individual countries and international institutions introduce measures to prevent crimes against humanity, as well as open more avenues to the domestic and international prosecution of war criminals.

The Evolving Laws of Genocide

In the aftermath of the serious crimes committed against civilians in the former Yugoslavia since 1991 and the Rwanda genocide of 1994, the United Nations Security Council created special international courts to bring the alleged perpetrators of these events to justice. While the UNGC stands as the standard definition of genocide in law, the new courts contributed significantly to today's nuanced meaning of genocide, crimes against humanity, ethnic cleansing, and serious war crimes in international criminal law.

Also helping to shape contemporary interpretations of such mass atrocity crimes are the special and mixed courts for Sierra Leone, Cambodia, Lebanon, and Iraq, which may be the last of their type in light of the creation of the International Criminal Court (ICC), with its broad jurisdiction over mass atrocity crimes in all countries that adhere to the Rome Statute of the ICC. The Yugoslavia and Rwanda tribunals have already clarified the law of genocide, ruling that rape can be prosecuted as a weapon in committing genocide, evidence of intent can be absent when convicting low-level perpetrators of genocide, and public incitement to commit genocide is a crime even if genocide does not immediately follow the incitement.

Several current controversies about genocide are worth noting and will require more research in the future:

1. Dictators accused of committing genocide or persecution may hold onto power more tightly for fear of becoming

vulnerable to prosecution after they step down. Therefore, do threats of international indictments of these alleged perpetrators actually delay transfers of power to more representative rulers, thereby causing needless suffering?

2. Would the large sum of money spent for international retributive justice be better spent on projects directly benefiting the survivors of genocide and persecution?

3. Can international courts render justice impartially or do they deliver only "victors' justice," that is the application of one set of rules to judge the vanquished and a different and laxer set of rules to judge the victors?

It is important to recognize that the law of genocide is constantly evolving, and scholars searching for the roots and early warning signs of genocide may prefer to use their own definitions of genocide in their work. While the UNGC stands as the standard definition of genocide in law, the debate over its interpretation and application will never end. The ultimate measure of the value of any definition of genocide is its utility for identifying the roots of genocide and preventing future genocides.

Motives for Genocide and Early Warning Signs

When identifying past cases of genocide, many scholars work with some version of the typology of motives published in 1990 by historian Frank Chalk and sociologist Kurt Jonassohn in their book *The History and Sociology of Genocide*. The authors identify the following four motives and acknowledge that they may overlap, or several lesser motives might also drive a perpetrator:

1. To eliminate a real or potential threat, as in Imperial Rome's decision to annihilate Carthage in 146 BC.

2. To spread terror among real or potential enemies, as in Genghis Khan's destruction of city-states and people who rebelled against the Mongols in the thirteenth century.

3. To acquire economic wealth, as in the case of the Massachusetts Puritans' annihilation of the native Pequot people in 1637.

4. To implement a belief, theory, or an ideology, as in the case of Germany's decision under Hitler and the Nazis to destroy completely the Jewish people of Europe from 1941 to 1945.

Although these motives represent differing goals, they share common early warning signs of genocide. A good example of genocide in recent times that could have been prevented through close attention to early warning signs was the genocide of 1994 inflicted on the people labeled as "Tutsi" in Rwanda. Between 1959 and 1963, the predominantly Hutu political parties in power stigmatized all Tutsi as members of a hostile racial group, violently forcing their leaders and many civilians into exile in neighboring countries through a series of assassinations and massacres. Despite systematic exclusion of Tutsi from service in the military, government security agencies, and public service, as well as systematic discrimination against them in higher education, hundreds of thousands of Tutsi did remain behind in Rwanda. Government-issued cards identified each Rwandan as Hutu or Tutsi.

A generation later, some Tutsi raised in refugee camps in Uganda and elsewhere joined together, first organizing politically and then militarily, to reclaim a place in their homeland. When the predominantly Tutsi Rwanda Patriotic Front invaded Rwanda from Uganda in October 1990, extremist Hutu political parties demonized all of Rwanda's Tutsi as traitors, ratcheting up hate propaganda through radio broadcasts on government-run Radio Rwanda and privately owned radio station RTLM. Within the print media, *Kangura* and other publications used vicious cartoons to further demonize Tutsi and to stigmatize any Hutu who dared advocate bringing Tutsi into the government. Massacres of dozens and later hundreds of Tutsi sprang up even as Rwandans prepared to elect a coalition government led by moderate political parties, and as the United Nations dispatched a small international military force led by Canadian general Roméo Dallaire to oversee the elections and political transition. Late in 1992, an international human rights organization's investigating team detected the hate propaganda campaign, verified systematic massacres of Tutsi, and warned the international community that Rwanda had already entered the early stages of genocide, to no avail. On April 6, 1994, Rwanda's genocidal killing accelerated at an alarming pace when someone shot down the airplane flying Rwandan president Juvenal Habyarimana home from peace talks in Arusha, Tanzania.

Hundreds of thousands of Tutsi civilians—including children, women, and the elderly—died horrible deaths because the world ignored the early warning signs of the genocide and refused to act. Prominent among those early warning signs were: 1) systematic, government-decreed discrimination against the Tutsi as members of a supposed racial group; 2) government-issued identity cards labeling every Tutsi as a member of a racial group; 3) hate propaganda casting all Tutsi as subversives and traitors; 4) organized assassinations and massacres targeting Tutsi; and 5) indoctrination of militias and special military units to believe that all Tutsi posed a genocidal threat to the existence of Hutu and would enslave Hutu if they ever again became the rulers of Rwanda.

Genocide Prevention and the Responsibility to Protect

The shock waves emanating from the Rwanda genocide forced world leaders at least to acknowledge in principle that the national sovereignty of offending nations cannot trump the responsibility of those governments to prevent the infliction of mass atrocities on their own people. When governments violate that obligation, the member states of the United Nations have a responsibility to get involved. Such involvement can take the form of, first, offering to help the local government change its ways

through technical advice and development aid, and second—
if the local government persists in assaulting its own people—
initiating armed intervention to protect the civilians at risk. In
2005 the United Nations began to implement the Responsibility
to Protect initiative, a framework of principles to guide the international community in preventing mass atrocities.

As in many real-world domains, theory and practice often
diverge. Genocide and crimes against humanity are rooted in
problems that produce failing states: poverty, poor education,
extreme nationalism, lawlessness, dictatorship, and corruption.
Implementing the principles of the Responsibility to Protect doc-
trine burdens intervening state leaders with the necessity of ad-
dressing each of those problems over a long period of time. And
when those problems prove too intractable and complex to solve
easily, the citizens of the intervening nations may lose patience,
voting out the leader who initiated the intervention. Arguments
based solely on humanitarian principles fail to overcome such
concerns. What is needed to persuade political leaders to stop
preventable mass atrocities are compelling arguments based on
their own national interests.

Preventable mass atrocities threaten the national interests of
all states in five specific ways:

1. Mass atrocities create conditions that engender widespread and concrete threats from terrorism, piracy, and
   other forms of lawlessness on the land and sea;
2. Mass atrocities facilitate the spread of warlordism, whose
   tentacles block affordable access to vital raw materials
   produced in the affected country and threaten the pros-
   perity of all nations that depend on the consumption of
   these resources;
3. Mass atrocities trigger cascades of refugees and internally
   displaced populations that, combined with climate change
   and growing international air travel, will accelerate the
   worldwide incidence of lethal infectious diseases;

4. Mass atrocities spawn single-interest parties and political agendas that drown out more diverse political discourse in the countries where the atrocities take place and in the countries that host large numbers of refugees. Xenophobia and nationalist backlashes are the predictable consequences of government indifference to mass atrocities elsewhere that could have been prevented through early actions;

5. Mass atrocities foster the spread of national and transnational criminal networks trafficking in drugs, women, arms, contraband, and laundered money.

Alerting elected political representatives to the consequences of mass atrocities should be part of every student movement's agenda in the twenty-first century. Adam Smith, the great political economist and author of *The Wealth of Nations*, put it best when he wrote: "It is not from the benevolence of the butcher, the brewer, or the baker that we expect our dinner, but from their regard to their own interest." Self-interest is a powerful engine for good in the marketplace and can be an equally powerful motive and source of inspiration for state action to prevent genocide and mass persecution. In today's new global village, the lives we save may be our own.

Frank Chalk

Frank Chalk, who has a doctorate from the University of Wisconsin-Madison, is a professor of history and director of the Montreal Institute for Genocide and Human Rights Studies at Concordia University in Montreal, Canada. He is coauthor, with Kurt

Jonassohn, of The History and Sociology of Genocide *(1990); coauthor with General Roméo Dallaire, Kyle Matthews, Carla Barqueiro, and Simon Doyle of* Mobilizing the Will to Intervene: Leadership to Prevent Mass Atrocities *(2010); and associate editor of the three-volume* Macmillan Reference USA Encyclopedia of Genocide and Crimes Against Humanity *(2004). Chalk served as president of the International Association of Genocide Scholars from June 1999 to June 2001. His current research focuses on the use of radio and television broadcasting in the incitement and prevention of genocide, and domestic laws on genocide. For more information on genocide and examples of the experiences of people displaced by genocide and other human rights violations, interested readers can consult the websites of the Montreal Institute for Genocide and Human Rights Studies (http://migs.concordia.ca) and the Montreal Life Stories project (www.lifestoriesmontreal.ca).*

World Map

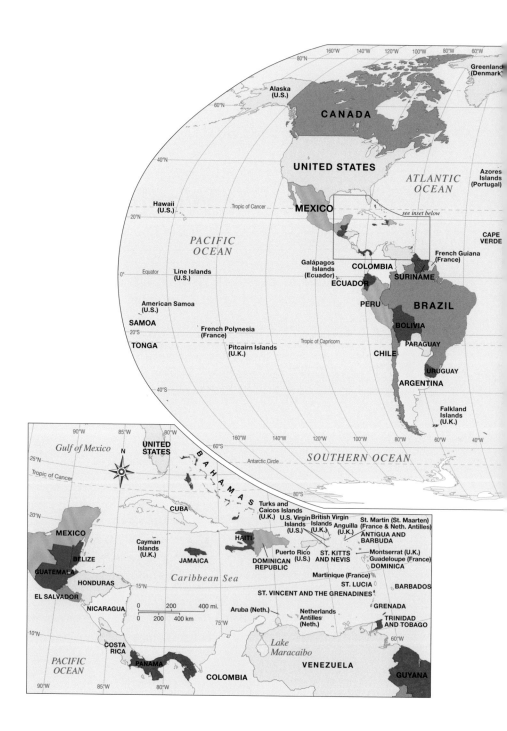

160°W 140°W 120°W 100°W 80°W 60°W

Greenland
(Denmark)

80°N

Alaska
(U.S.)

60°N

CANADA

40°N

UNITED STATES

ATLANTIC
OCEAN

Azores
Islands
(Portugal)

Hawaii
(U.S.)

Tropic of Cancer

20°N

MEXICO

see inset below

CAPE
VERDE

PACIFIC
OCEAN

Galápagos
Islands
(Ecuador)

COLOMBIA

French Guiana
(France)

0°

Equator

Line Islands
(U.S.)

ECUADOR

SURINAME

American Samoa
(U.S.)

PERU

BRAZIL

SAMOA

French Polynesia
(France)

BOLIVIA

20°S

TONGA

Pitcairn Islands
(U.K.)

Tropic of Capricorn

PARAGUAY

CHILE

URUGUAY

ARGENTINA

40°S

Falkland
Islands
(U.K.)

160°W 140°W 120°W 100°W 80°W 60°W 40°W

60°S

Antarctic Circle

SOUTHERN OCEAN

80°S

90°W 85°W 80°W

Gulf of Mexico

N

UNITED
STATES

B
A
H
A
M
A
S

25°N

Tropic of Cancer

CUBA

Turks and
Caicos Islands
(U.K.)

U.S. Virgin British Virgin
Islands Islands
(U.S.) (U.K.)

Anguilla
(U.K.)

St. Martin (St. Maarten)
(France & Neth. Antilles)

ANTIGUA AND
BARBUDA

20°N

MEXICO

Cayman
Islands
(U.K.)

HAITI

Puerto Rico
(U.S.)

ST. KITTS
AND NEVIS

Montserrat (U.K.)
Guadeloupe (France)
DOMINICA

BELIZE

JAMAICA

DOMINICAN
REPUBLIC

GUATEMALA

Caribbean Sea

Martinique (France)

ST. LUCIA

BARBADOS

HONDURAS

15°N

ST. VINCENT AND THE GRENADINES

EL SALVADOR

0 200 400 mi.

NICARAGUA

0 200 400 km

75°W

Aruba (Neth.)

Netherlands
Antilles
(Neth.)

GRENADA

TRINIDAD
AND TOBAGO

10°N

COSTA
RICA

Lake
Maracaibo

PACIFIC
OCEAN

PANAMA

COLOMBIA

VENEZUELA

GUYANA

90°W 85°W 80°W 60°W

| 16

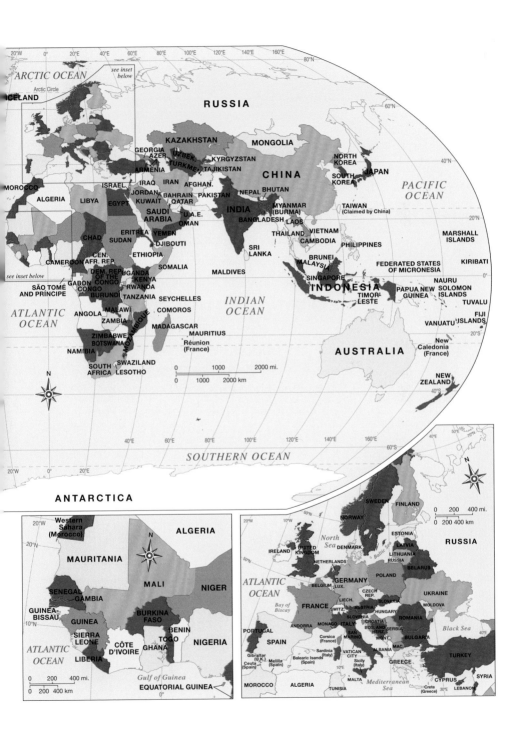

20°W 0° 20°E 40°E 60°E 80°E 100°E 120°E 140°E 160°E 80°N

ARCTIC OCEAN

see inset below

ICELAND

Arctic Circle

RUSSIA

60°N

KAZAKHSTAN   MONGOLIA

GEORGIA   NORTH   40°N
AZER. UZBEK.   KYRGYZSTAN   KOREA
ARMENIA TURKMEN. TAJIKISTAN   CHINA   SOUTH   JAPAN
                                                                  KOREA   PACIFIC
MOROCCO   ISRAEL IRAQ IRAN AFGHAN.   NEPAL BHUTAN   OCEAN
                JORDAN BAHRAIN PAKISTAN   TAIWAN   20°N
ALGERIA LIBYA EGYPT KUWAIT QATAR   (Claimed by China)
                SAUDI   U.A.E.   INDIA MYANMAR
                ARABIA OMAN   BANGLADESH (BURMA)
                                                LAOS
                ERITREA YEMEN   THAILAND VIETNAM   MARSHALL
        CHAD SUDAN   DJIBOUTI   CAMBODIA   ISLANDS
                                            SRI   PHILIPPINES
CAMEROON CEN. ETHIOPIA   LANKA   BRUNEI
        AFR. REP.   SOMALIA   MALAYSIA   FEDERATED STATES   KIRIBATI
see inset below DEM. REP. UGANDA   MALDIVES   SINGAPORE   OF MICRONESIA
SÃO TOMÉ GABON OF THE KENYA   NAURU
AND PRÍNCIPE CONGO RWANDA   INDONESIA   PAPUA NEW SOLOMON   0°
            BURUNDI TANZANIA SEYCHELLES   TIMOR- GUINEA ISLANDS
ATLANTIC ANGOLA MALAWI   COMOROS   INDIAN   LESTE   TUVALU
OCEAN   ZAMBIA   OCEAN   FIJI
        ZIMBABWE   MADAGASCAR   VANUATU ISLANDS
        BOTSWANA   MAURITIUS   20°S
NAMIBIA   Réunion   AUSTRALIA   New
        SOUTH SWAZILAND (France)   Caledonia
        AFRICA LESOTHO   0   1000   2000 mi.   (France)
                                                                  NEW
                          0 1000 2000 km   ZEALAND 40°S

N

40°E 60°E 80°E 100°E 120°E 140°E 160°E
                                              60°S

SOUTHERN OCEAN

20°W 0° 20°E

ANTARCTICA

20°W Western   ALGERIA   20°W 10°W   SWEDEN FINLAND   0   200   400 mi.
      Sahara   NORWAY
      (Morocco) 20°N   North   0 200 400 km
                                                    Sea   ESTONIA   RUSSIA
MAURITANIA   N   IRELAND UNITED DENMARK Baltic Sea LATVIA
                                          KINGDOM   Sea   LITHUANIA
                MALI   NIGER   ATLANTIC   NETHERLANDS RUSSIA
                                 OCEAN BELGIUM GERMANY POLAND BELARUS
SENEGAL   LUX.
GAMBIA   Bay of FRANCE CZECH   SLOVAKIA UKRAINE
GUINEA-   BURKINA   Biscay   LIECH. REP.
BISSAU   FASO   ANDORRA SWITZ. AUSTRIA HUNGARY MOLDOVA
    GUINEA   BENIN   MONACO ITALY SLOVENIA CROATIA ROMANIA
SIERRA   TOGO   PORTUGAL SAN BOS. AND SERBIA Black Sea
LEONE CÔTE GHANA NIGERIA   SPAIN   MARINO HERZ. MONT. BULGARIA
    D'IVOIRE   Corsica   MAC.
LIBERIA   (France) VATICAN ALBANIA   TURKEY
ATLANTIC   Gibraltar Sardinia CITY
OCEAN   (U.K.) Melilla (Italy) Sicily GREECE
    0   200   400 mi.   Ceuta (Spain) Balearic Isands (Italy) CYPRUS SYRIA
                                 (Spain) (Spain)   Crete
    0 200 400 km Gulf of Guinea MOROCCO ALGERIA Mediterranean (Greece) LEBANON
EQUATORIAL GUINEA   TUNISIA Sea
                                 MALTA

Chronology

1933	King Mohammed Zahir Shah takes the throne as ruler of Afghanistan.
1964	The constitution of Afghanistan proclaims legal equality for women.
July 17, 1973	King Zahir Shah is peacefully overthrown by his cousin, former Prime Minister Mohammed Daoud Khan. Daoud converts Afghanistan from a monarchy to a democratic republic.
April 28, 1978	A Marxist-Leninist military coup—the Saur Revolution—begins with the assassination of President Daoud. The Communist People's Democratic Party of Afghanistan comes to power.
December 24, 1979	Soviet troops invade Afghanistan, sparking mujahideen resistance.
1980	Seventy thousand Afghan troops abandon the Soviet-controlled Afghan army in favor of joining mujahideen fighters.
February 1986	Soviet premier Mikhail Gorbachev voices a desire to pull troops from Afghanistan.
February 15, 1989	Final Soviet troops are withdrawn.

1991	The Communist government of Afghanistan collapses. Fighting continues among mujahideen militias.
1992	A mujahideen government takes power in Kabul. President Mohammad Najibullah—the last Soviet-installed Afghan president—takes refuge in the United Nations' Kabul offices.
1992–1996	Afghanistan is embroiled in a civil war, with an estimated 3 million casualties.
1993	Tens of thousands of Afghans die as a result of ongoing feuds between mujahideen commanders.
1994	The Taliban begins to gain popular support in Afghanistan.
1995–1996	The Taliban conquers Kandahar, Herat, Jalalabad, and Kabul. Members of the Taliban capture and execute former President Najibullah.
September 1996	The Taliban begins its rule of Afghanistan.
1998	Saudi-born al Qaeda terrorist leader Osama bin Laden bombs US embassies in Kenya and Tanzania. Taliban spiritual leader Mullah Mohammed Omar offers Bin Laden sanctuary in Afghanistan.

September 11, 2001	Followers of Osama bin Laden crash airplanes into the World Trade Center in New York City, the Pentagon in Washington, DC, and a field in Pennsylvania, killing nearly three thousand people.
October 2001	The United States launches air strikes targeting al Qaeda and Taliban operations in Afghanistan. A US invasion follows.
	Taliban rule ends; US occupation begins.
2004	The Islamic Republic of Afghanistan is formed with popularly elected president Hamid Karzai (a US ally) as its leader.

CHAPTER 1

Historical Background on Afghanistan

Chapter Exercises

Source: *The World Factbook*. Washington, DC: Central Intelligence Agency, 2012. www.cia.gov.

STATISTICS

	Afghanistan
Total Area	652,230 sq km (251,827 sq mi) World ranking: 41
Population	30,419,928 (July 2012 est.) World ranking: 40
Ethnic Groups	42% Pashtun, 27% Tajik, 9% Hazara, 9% Uzbek, 4% Aimak, 3% Turkmen, 2% Baloch, 4% other
Languages	50%Afghan Persian/Dari (official), 35% Pashto (official), 11% Turkic languages (primarily Uzbek and Turkmen), 4% 30 minor languages (primarily Balochi, Pashai, Nuristani, and Pamiri)
Religions	80% Sunni Muslim, 19% Shia Muslim, 1% other
Infant Mortality	121.63 deaths/1,000 live births World ranking: 1
Average Years of Education	9 years Male: 11 years Female: 7 years
Literacy (total population)	28.1% Male: 43.1% Female: 12.6% (2000 est.)
Median Afghan Age	17.9 years
Life Expectancy	49.71 years World ranking: 217
GDP	$30.11 billion (2011 est.) World ranking: 110

1. **Analyzing Statistics**

   Question 1: Compare Afghanistan's gross domestic product (GDP) with the $15.29 trillion GDP of the United States. While Afghanistan has been invaded and occupied several times in recent history, no foreign invader has been truly successful in taking over this nation. Is it surprising, given their meager resources, that the Afghan people have consistently resisted foreign invasions? Why is Afghanistan sometimes called "the graveyard of empires"?

   Question 2: Consider the average age of an Afghan, his or her access to education, the infant mortality rate in Afghanistan, and the life expectancy of the average Afghan. Do wealthier nations have any obligation to the people of Afghanistan? What actions should be taken to aid Afghanistan?

   Question 3: Consider the statistics regarding ethnic, religious, and linguistic groups in Afghanistan. What role do you think Afghan diversity played during the Soviet occupation and US invasion?

2. **Writing Prompt**

   Write an article describing the August 1986 attack on the village of Garabad in Konduz Province. Give your article a compelling title and not only inform readers of the facts of the event, but also elicit an emotional response.

3. **Group Activity**

   Break into small groups randomly assigned to be sympathetic to the Soviet Union, the United States, or the Afghan people. Debate whether the United Nations' position—as presented in its 1986 resolution—represented an appropriate and effective response to Soviet military action in Afghanistan; if not, how should the United Nations have responded?

Three Decades of Human Rights Abuses in Afghanistan: An Overview

Patricia Gossman

Patricia Gossman is an independent human rights consultant specializing in Afghanistan and a former senior researcher on South Asia for Human Rights Watch. In 2001 she launched the Afghanistan Justice Project, which documents past human rights abuses in Afghanistan. In the following viewpoint, Gossman offers a history of human rights abuses and war crimes in Afghanistan, beginning with the rise of the People's Democratic Party of Afghanistan (a Communist political movement) in 1978 and continuing through the period of Taliban rule, the post–9/11 US military presence, and the rise of the current government led by Hamid Karzai. Gossman asserts that throughout this more than thirty-year period, the United States often funneled money to Afghans known to have committed atrocities, and war criminals and serial human rights abusers continue to be active in Afghan political life.

Conflict has raged in Afghanistan since April 1978. It has been marked by brutality on a massive scale. Although the major fighting ended with the defeat of the Taliban in 2001, conflict continues especially in the south and east of the country, and many of those responsible for war crimes in earlier phases of the war continue to wield power. During every phase of the fighting, Afghan and foreign armed factions committed crimes against humanity and serious war crimes. These included large-scale massacres, disappearances and summary executions of tens of thousands of Afghans, indiscriminate bombing and rocketing that killed hundreds of thousands of civilians, torture, mass rape and other atrocities. There has never been any serious effort, international or domestic, to account for these crimes.

A Failed "Social Revolution"

Afghanistan's quarter-century of war began on April 27, 1978, when the People's Democratic Party of Afghanistan (PDPA), a small, Marxist-Leninist [Communist] party, launched a coup, overthrowing and killing then-President Mohammed Daoud Khan and most of his family. The PDPA then embarked on an ambitious and ruthless campaign to transform Afghanistan into a modern socialist state. Mass arrests and executions began shortly after the coup. Among the thousands of victims were individuals (or entire families) that the new regime considered as potential opponents: leaders of social, political, or religious groups, professionals of every kind and other members of the educated class.

Lacking popular support to carry out its political agenda, the PDPA found itself in a situation spiraling out of control. The repression sparked uprisings throughout the country and mutinies within the Afghan army that threatened to destabilize the regime. The disintegration of the army marked a turning point for Soviet policy and led to the [Soviet] decision to invade [Afghanistan] on December 25, 1979, ostensibly in response to a request for military support from the exiled deputy prime minister Babrak [Karmal], who was then installed as a puppet leader.

A group of Muslim rebel fighters—engaged in conflict with Marxist Afghan government troops—pose with weapons in December 1979. A Communist takeover of the Afghan government in 1978 was followed by several decades of internal instability marked by violence and atrocities on all sides. © AP Images/Steve McCurry.

The Soviet "Scorched Earth" Campaign

The Soviet occupation brought about a shift in tactics in the war as the resistance forces began to coalesce around a number of factions largely organized along ethnic lines. They did not control the cities, but moved mainly in the rural areas where they enjoyed popular support. Most of the factions maintained headquarters or political representatives in Pakistan or Iran, where they also established conduits for vast amounts of military assistance that began to flow principally from the U.S. through Pakistan. Aware that the mass arrests and executions carried out earlier by the PDPA had only fueled the resistance and nearly destroyed the Army, the Soviets employed more systematic means of intelligence gathering. The secret police, the KhAD, was modeled on the Soviet KGB [security agency]. It engaged in widespread summary executions, detentions and torture of suspected mujahidin (resistance) supporters. Torture survivors from this period whom I have interviewed regularly identified Soviet personnel supervising the torture.

In the countryside, Soviet forces bombed routinely and indiscriminately; the aim was both to demoralize the civilian population supporting the resistance and to destroy its means of providing food and shelter to the mujahidin. Thus, irrigation systems, cropland and other rural resources were bombed as well as villages. The bombing killed countless civilians and devastated the countryside. From the early 1980s on, most refugees arriving in Pakistan reported they had fled because of the bombing. In all, some five million Afghans fled the country. In addition to the bombing, Soviet and Afghan forces carried out reprisals against civilians, executing any they believed to support the resistance. Soviet forces also sowed mines throughout the country; many remain a threat to Afghans living in rural areas today.

The Rise of Afghan Warlords

Desertions from the Afghan army had so decimated the military that Soviet forces and advisors were deployed in great numbers;

Soviet personnel made decisions for the state, and for the PDPA officials who nominally governed it. Thus, some responsibility for war crimes committed during this period may rest with those Soviet officers as well as with senior Afghan officials. The members of the politburos of the two countries' ruling parties could also be held accountable for the decisions and policies during this period. No one knows how many Afghans died in the ten years following the revolution, but the number may be as high as one million.

In February 1986 the Soviet Union, under President [Mikhail] Gorbachev, reached a decision to withdraw its forces by the end of 1988. The head of KhAD, Najibullah, was "elected" general secretary of the PDPA and subsequently became president of the Revolutionary Council. The Geneva Accords, outlining the provisions of the Soviet withdrawal, were signed on April 14, 1988, by Afghanistan, Pakistan, the U.S. and the USSR. Military and economic aid from the U.S. and USSR continued to their respective clients.

Without the Soviet army, the Najibullah government increasingly relied for its defense on regional militias, paying for their loyalty with Soviet-provided cash and weapons. Although some were regular army divisions, the militias operated outside [the] ordinary chain of command within the military, and were largely autonomous within their areas of control. Militia forces were responsible for waylaying and robbing travelers, including returning refugees, extorting money from traders, kidnapping, looting property, forcibly taking land, and planting mines without mapping or marking them.

Ethnic Strife and Islamist Militias

A number of mujahidin groups also committed war crimes during this period. Many of those based in Pakistan who had the support of Pakistani military and intelligence agencies operated with impunity and had considerable control over the Afghan refugee population. One of the most powerful of these was Hizb-i

Islami, headed by Gulbuddin Hekmatyar. These mujahidin carried out assassinations and maintained secret detention facilities in Pakistan; persons detained there included Afghan refugees who opposed the mujahidin leaders, or who worked for foreign NGOs, especially those employing women.

The demise of the Soviet Union meant the end of Soviet aid, and of the Najibullah regime. When the Najibullah government collapsed in April 1992, Kabul was engulfed in civil war as the multiple factions that had participated in the struggle against the PDPA regime and the Soviet occupation, along with the militias, fought for control of territory. Despite efforts by the UN and some of the neighboring countries to mediate, there was no agreement on a power-sharing settlement. The factional fighting fell largely along ethnic lines, and groups frequently targeted civilians from rival ethnic groups.

In many cases, the atrocities were carried out on the orders or with the direct knowledge of senior commanders and party leaders. However, senior commanders secured the loyalty of their subordinates at a cost, and operated with the knowledge that any effort to weaken the power of the commanders under them might lead them to switch sides, taking their troops with them. While this fact does not absolve the leaders of responsibility for the actions of their forces, it is critical in understanding command and control within the armed factions.

Chaos Rages in Kabul Despite a Cease-Fire Agreement

On April 26, 1992, most of the party leaders in Pakistan announced that they had reached agreement on an interim government that would hold power until a council could be convened and elections subsequently held. As defense minister of the new government, Ahmad Shah Massoud attempted to gain control first of Kabul itself—an objective that eluded him for three years. His principal foe was Hizb-i Islami, whose rocket attacks killed thousands of civilians between 1992 and 1995. Every major armed faction in Kabul had an arsenal of heavy weaponry that they used in battles that raged in the streets of Kabul during this period. Rape, as well as other targeted attacks on civilians, was ethnically based. In many cases, it was used as a means of ethnic cleansing. In one of the most notorious incidents of the civil war, hundreds of ethnic Shia Hazaras were raped and killed in a February 1993 massacre. Survivors I have spoken to identified commanders responsible for the killings and rape who continue to operate with impunity in Kabul. The leader of one of the factions responsible, Abdul Rasul Sayyaf, was elected to parliament in September 2005.

The Taliban Rises to National Prominence

The Taliban emerged out of the chaos of the post–1992 period. In this group's first successful military operation, the Taliban disarmed and executed a notoriously predatory commander in Kandahar. The Taliban moved on to take on other commanders and very quickly attracted the support of Pakistan, who needed a client it thought would protect Pakistan's interests. By 1995 the Taliban took control of Herat, and in 1996, Kabul. The Taliban's actions with respect to women have been well documented, as they imposed harsh restrictions on girls' schools and employment for women.

The Taliban were highly centralized, with regional governors in all strategic provinces reporting directly to the group's leader, Mullah Omar. The influence of non-Afghans over Mullah Omar increased after Osama bin Laden returned to Afghanistan in 1996 and in 1997 moved to Kandahar.

In May 1997 the largest single massacre of the war took place. Mainly Uzbek troops under General Malik Pahlawan captured over 3,000 Taliban soldiers at Mazar-i-Sharif and executed them. Some were taken to a desert location and shot; others were thrown down wells. One of the few survivors described to me how he crawled from under the bodies until he reached a village where the residents were willing to shelter him. Gen. Malik continues to live in Kabul.

The United States Invades Afghanistan

The major war crimes of the Taliban were committed between 1997 and 2001 as they moved outside their ethnic Pashtun heartland. In areas where they encountered resistance, Taliban forces responded by massacring civilians and other noncombatants, and burning down villages. In August 1998, they massacred at least 2,000 people, mainly Hazara civilians, in Mazar-i-Sharif, exacting what they said was revenge for the massacre of their own troops the previous year. In July 1999, the Taliban launched a major offensive across the plain north of Kabul known as Shamali (meaning "North"), summarily executing civilians, and burning down villages, fields and orchards. The devastation was incalculable. In both of these operations, the Taliban had considerable support from Pakistan.

When the United States intervened in Afghanistan in late 2001, its forces sought allies on the ground among the commanders of the so-called "Northern Alliance" opposed to the Taliban. The U.S.'s overriding objective in Afghanistan was to defeat [the militant Islamist organization] al-Qaeda and remove the Taliban from power with minimal U.S. casualties. The fact that many of these new allies had records that included not only grave breaches of international humanitarian law, but in some cases criminal ties to narcotics trafficking and other illicit activities, apparently posed no obstacle. The U.S. provided arms, cash and other support to commanders whom it believed could keep the Taliban and al-Qaeda at bay. But the U.S. failed to achieve that objective. Although a new central government was established under President Hamid Karzai in 2002, the Taliban remain a lethal force, with support flowing across the border from the "tribal areas" of Pakistan. Meanwhile a number of the commanders the U.S. has backed have strengthened their positions against rivals, and have continued to engage in abuse and criminal activities.

The Fall of the Taliban

In mid-November, 2001, Northern Alliance forces surrounded the last Taliban stronghold in Kunduz. When the Taliban forces

A Thumbnail History of Modern Afghanistan

The Afghan nation began to emerge in the late eighteenth century. It was ruled, with brief interruptions, by a succession of monarchs whose consolidation of power was constantly undermined by civil wars and foreign invasions. The current borders of Afghanistan were delineated in the nineteenth century, as a result of the "great game" rivalry between Russia and Britain. Britain exerted some influence over Afghan foreign policy from the late nineteenth century until the Third Anglo-Afghan War in 1919. Afghanistan joined the UN in 1946.

In 1973, King Zahir Shah was overthrown in a coup by his cousin and former Prime Minister, Muhammad Daud. Daud declared Afghanistan a republic, with himself as president, and the King went into exile in Italy.

and the Pakistani and Arab fighters with them surrendered, thousands were taken into custody and transported to prison facilities under the control of General [Abdul Rashid] Dostum at Shiberghan and Qala-i-Jangi, near Mazar-i-Sharif. At least two hundred detainees (and, according to some sources, many more) reportedly died en route in the overcrowded container trucks used to transport them and were buried in mass graves in the desert area of Dasht-i-Leili near Shiberghan. Gen. Dostum later acknowledged that some two hundred prisoners had suffocated due to inadvertent overcrowding. A full investigation of the incident has never taken place.

Not all Afghan commanders and leaders involved in the long years of conflict engaged in war crimes; many should enjoy the right to participate in politics. However, too many with criminal records have secured places in political office or security agencies. By allying itself—for the sake of political expediency—with local commanders with long records of past crimes, the U.S. has

Daud's government, however, was opposed by both the leftist People's Democratic Party of Afghanistan (PDPA) and traditional ethnic leaders. In April 1978, leftist military officers overthrew and killed Daud and PDPA leader Noor Muhammad Taraki became President.

Late in 1978, Islamic traditionalists and ethnic leaders began an armed revolt, and by the summer of 1979 they controlled much of Afghanistan's rural areas. In September, Taraki was deposed and later killed. He was replaced by his deputy, Hafizullah Amin, but Amin also failed to suppress the rebellion, and the government's position weakened. On 25 December 1979, Soviet forces entered Afghanistan, and took control of Kabul. Babrak Karmal, leader of a less hard-line faction of the PDPA, became President. Karmal adopted more open policies towards religion and ethnicity. However, the rebellion intensified.

"Afghanistan and the United Nations," United Nations News Centre, April 18, 2012. www.un.org.

jeopardized prospects for establishing stable and accountable institutions in Afghanistan, and has helped reinforce a pattern of impunity that undermines the legitimacy of the political process.

U.S. Forces Abuse Afghans

U.S. forces have also committed grave abuses. These have included crude and brutal methods of torture that have sometimes led to death, the use of secret detention facilities that facilitate torture; and unacknowledged detentions that are tantamount to disappearances, in violation of prohibitions on prolonged arbitrary detention in customary international humanitarian law and human rights law. During Cherif Bassiouni's tenure as UN Independent Expert on Human Rights in Afghanistan, the U.S. blocked his efforts to inspect U.S. detention facilities. Bassiouni had particularly condemned the United States' use of "firebases" to hold detainees—facilities not accessible to the ICRC [International Committee of the Red Cross]. Under U.S.

pressure, in 2005 the UN Human Rights Commission did not renew Bassiouni's mandate.

In January 2005, the Afghan Independent Human Rights Commission published the results of a national survey which showed overwhelming support for measures to keep war criminals out of power and to begin a truth process to account for past crimes. Before the September 2005 parliamentary elections, an electoral complaint commission received hundreds of submissions from Afghans charging candidates with war crimes and human rights violations. The fact that many candidates known to have illegal militias were not removed from the ballot was seen as one factor in the low voter turnout. After months of delay, in December 2005, the cabinet of President Hamid Karzai's administration adopted an action plan on transitional justice that was based on the Human Rights Commission's recommendations. A year later, few of the recommended steps had taken place. While some Afghans see the need to find a way to address the past, others, as well as some senior U.S. officials, argue that rocking the boat will lead to greater instability. In fact, the failure to scrutinize the records of those vying for power has led to the entrenchment of persons who continue to terrorize civilians and otherwise undermine the political process.

The Soviet Union Explains Its Intervention in Afghanistan

Boris Gromov

Boris Gromov was a decorated soldier in Afghanistan during the Soviet occupation. In his 1994 book, Limited Contingent, *Gromov examines the experience of the "limited contingent" of Soviet soldiers sent to Afghanistan, which initially numbered at least eighty thousand. In the following viewpoint, taken from* Limited Contingent, *Gromov reprints an internal document sent from the Central Committee of the Communist Party of the Soviet Union (CC CPSU) to Soviet ambassadors around the world. The document explains the position of the Soviet Union following the April 1978 Communist revolution in Afghanistan (now called the Saur Revolution) and the subsequent political strife. The CC CPSU blamed this instability on external pressure from the United States, Pakistan, and China.*

D ear comrades!
  Following the tradition which has developed in relations between our Parties, the CC CPSU [Central Committee of the Communist Party of the Soviet Union] would like to share

Boris Gromov, "Circular Cable to Soviet Ambassadors in Non-Fraternal Countries with Official Soviet Position Regarding Developments of the Situation Around Afghanistan," December 27, 1979, Cold War International History Project (CWIHP). www.CWIHP .org. Translated for CWIHP by Gary Goldberg. Reprinted by permission of the Woodrow Wilson International Center for Scholars.

A Look at Afghanistan's Communist Leaders

Afghanistan entered its current age of perpetual upheaval in 1973, when the standing monarch, King Mohammed Zahir Shah, was overthrown in a bloodless coup by his cousin, former Afghan prime minister Mohammed Daoud Khan. Rather than declaring himself king, Daoud established Afghanistan as a republic, with himself as president. Unfortunately, both the radical political left (specifically the Communist PDPA, or People's Democratic Party of Afghanistan) and conservative traditional tribal leaders opposed the progressive government. On April 28, 1978 Daoud was assassinated in a political coup by the PDPA and replaced with the founder of the PDPA, Nur Muhammad Taraki. Thus began the Saur Revolution, which marks the rise of the Communist Democratic Republic of Afghanistan.

Taraki's radical Communist policies—which included equal rights for women, a push for universal literacy within Afghanistan, and land reforms limiting how much property a family could hold—proved violently unpopular with tribal elders and their followers. Riots, uprisings by the mujahideen (Muslim guerilla fighters), and mass desertions from the Afghan army ensued. Taraki responded

with the leaders of your Party our views and an assessment of recent events in Afghanistan.

As you well know, a new progressive national [political] system was created in Afghanistan as a result of the April 1978 Revolution. Much work was done in the country to eliminate the despotic monarchy by enlisting the broad popular masses on the side of the Revolution; land reform has been carried out, and a large amount of land has been transferred to the working peasantry; the payment of kalym (compensation) for a bride has been abolished; and other reforms have been carried out in the interests of the people.

with air raids and artillery. Despite repeated requests, the Soviet Union was unwilling to offer Taraki military assistance. He was overthrown and executed within a year by his former minister of foreign affairs and partner in the revolution, Hafizullah Amin.

But Amin was likewise unable to control the revolt, which was now developing into civil war. In 1979 the Soviet Union intervened in Afghanistan, sending in tens of thousands of ground troops with air support, and effectively occupying Afghanistan. Soviet officials accused Amin of being a CIA pawn and assassinated Amin and his family before the end of the year. Amin's entire rule lasted less than three months.

The Soviet Union replaced Amin with Babrak Karmal (who had served in a role similar to vice president under Taraki). Karmal favored the USSR (which had long held that a stable, allied Afghanistan was vital to their security), but he was unable to win over the Afghan people. The Soviets ultimately replaced him with Mohammad Najibullah in 1986. Najibullah was the former head of the notorious KHAD, the Afghan secret police. He served as president with strong Soviet backing, but little popular support, until the Communist government collapsed and mujahideen took the capital, Kabul, in 1992. Najibullah spent the next four years hiding in Afghanistan's United Nations headquarters. When the Taliban gained control of the country in 1996, they arrested Najibullah, castrated him, dragged him behind a truck through the streets of Kabul, and then publicly hanged him.

However the revolutionary events in Afghanistan have met with fierce opposition on the part of hostile foreign reactionary forces. Constant subversive activity from Pakistan, Iran, and China has been unleashed. In turn, the reactionary remnants of the old regime, landowners deprived of land, the former minions of the monarchy, and part of the Muslim clergy have unleashed a struggle against the revolutionary order.

Dissatisfaction with President Hafizullah Amin

To this was added the mistaken, it must be frankly said, dictatorial, despotic actions of [Hafizullah] Amin, violations of elementary norms of legality, widespread repression of every-one who did not agree with him, including those who for many years fought against the monarchy and actively participated in the April Revolution.

Having eliminated the former General Secretary of the People's Democratic Party and President of the Republic [Nur Muhammad] Taraki, H. Amin has recently hypocritically talked of humaneness and legality, given ultrarevolutionary speeches, etc., but in fact has carried out massive repression and under-mined the foundations of the revolutionary order.

Thus external intervention and terror against honest per-sons devoted to the cause of the Revolution and the interests of the people has created a threat of liquidation of what the April Revolution brought the Afghan people.

As a result of the harmful and impermissible acts of H. Amin and his closest associates, enormous discontent and protests against the policy of H. Amin have arisen in the country and at the same time subversive activity of reactionaries has revived and attacks of armed formations sent from abroad have intensified.

Foreign Manipulation of the Situation in Afghanistan

All this has been exploited by foreign reactionary forces. They have intensified the infiltration of sizable armed groups (mainly from Pakistani territory), they have supplied various military formations with weapons and money, etc.; in a word, they have worked towards establishing the previous reactionary regime and subordinating Afghanistan to imperialism. American impe-rialism and the CIA, and also the Beijing leadership have acted as the main force in carrying out this policy.

However in Afghanistan there have been found forces which have risen decisively against the regime of H. Amin, removed him from power, and created new governing bodies for the Party and the country. Those who for many years fought against the monarchy and brought about the April Revolution together with

Soviet tanks fill a street in downtown Kabul, Afghanistan, in January 1981. The USSR said it would send a "limited" military presence and withdraw its troops as soon as the situation stabilized. However, the Soviet occupation of Afghanistan lasted for almost a decade. © Bettmann/Corbis.

Taraki have been brought into them. Karmal Babrak [sic] has become the head of the Party and the government. His speeches and appeals to the people of Afghanistan are directed at ensuring the national independence of Afghanistan; rallying the people together; carrying out a progressive, democratic policy; observing legality; establishing firm law and order; and [having] a humane attitude toward people. The new leadership is setting as its task the assurance of civic peace in the country. All of this gives reason to say that such a leadership will facilitate the strengthening of the People's Democratic Party of Afghanistan and a progressive republican system.

Afghanistan Requests Military Aid from the Soviet Union

The new government and Party leadership has turned to the USSR with a request to give it political and material aid, including military support.

The Soviet Union has decided to give this support. In this matter the Soviet and Afghan governments have relied on an international treaty concluded between the USSR and Afghanistan on 5 December 1978. Chapter 4 of this treaty says:

> The High Contracting Parties, acting in the spirit of the traditions of friendship and neighborliness and also the UN Charter, will consult and with the consent of both Parties undertake the appropriate measures to ensure the security, independence, and territorial integrity of both countries. They will continue to collaborate in the military field in the interests of strengthening the defensive ability of the High Contracting Parties.

The Soviet Union has given consent to the Afghan government to the introduction of a small military contingent for a period of time. Its very presence in Afghanistan will serve as a guarantee (barrier) against sudden armed attacks of hostile foreign forces (mainly from Pakistan) and from the actions of internal counterrevolutionary forces.

The Soviet armed formation will be withdrawn from Afghanistan as soon as the situation there stabilizes and the reasons which prompted this action no longer exist.

In taking this decision, the CC CPSU considered the possible negative reaction of imperialist states and their mass media. But the political attacks of class and ideological enemies should not deter the CPSU and the Soviet Union from granting the request of the Afghan leadership.

The CC CPSU expresses confidence that your Party will well understand the motives which dictated the need to give this kind of aid to democratic Afghanistan and will support these measures.

With Communist greetings,
THE CENTRAL COMMITTEE OF THE
COMMUNIST PARTY OF THE SOVIET UNION

The Afghan Government Reacts to US President Jimmy Carter's State of the Union Address

The Democratic Republic of Afghanistan

The following viewpoint was released by the Communist government of Afghanistan on February 14, 1980. It is drawn from The Truth About Afghanistan: Documents, Facts and Eyewitness Reports, *one of many anthologies of propaganda published by the Novosti Press Agency, the leading state-controlled Soviet news agency during the Cold War. In this document, the Soviet-controlled Afghan government indignantly responds to President Jimmy Carter's January 23, 1980, State of the Union address, in which Carter characterized the Soviet presence in Afghanistan as an "[attempt] to subjugate the fiercely independent and deeply religious people of Afghanistan." The Soviet government consistently claimed that operations in Afghanistan were largely peaceful and humanitarian, downplaying the massive scale of this military operation and Afghan resistance.*

On January 23, [1980] President Jimmy Carter addressed the American Congress with his State of the Union message. Having familiarised ourselves with this speech, we can only express our indignation and protest against the interpretation of events in Afghanistan and the surrounding region which the

Democratic Republic of Afghanistan, "Resolute Condemnation: A Protest by the Government of the Democratic Republic of Afghanistan," Kabul, February 14, 1980.

head of the American administration has put forward in this document. It completely disregards the true state of affairs and distorts events to the point when they cease to be recognisable.

The United States Interferes in Afghan Affairs

Essentially, the American President, without any grounds for doing so, has taken upon himself the right to decide for the Afghan people and its state leadership what is good and what is bad for our country, what kind of regime we should have, and what policies we should follow.

Such declarations represent nothing other than a continuation of the grave interference in the internal affairs of our nation. The President has taken the liberty of alleging that the popular rising against the despotic regime of Hafizullah Amin, which put an end to the bloody repressions and persecution of honest patriots, signified the "abolition of independence in Afghanistan". To make such a declaration is grossly to distort the facts.

In actual fact, as a result of the overthrow of the dictatorship of Hafizullah Amin, the attempt to turn Afghanistan into a bridgehead for aggressive actions against other countries was frustrated and our nation's sovereignty, independence and territorial integrity were protected against the interminable armed encroachments from beyond our borders.

The Soviet Union Is Protecting Afghanistan from US Encroachment

Is it not clear that this represents a revival and a strengthening of our independence, rather than an "abolition"?

What possible grounds can the President of the USA have for taking upon himself the right to choose a government for our people? Absolutely none!

This is the sovereign right of the Afghan people and only they are able to decide what kind of government suits them best.

And they made their choice at the time of the April revolution and the events of December 27, 1979.

Marchers at a demonstration in Moscow carry a large sign that reads "an end to imperialistic meddling in Afghanistan"—a reaction to the announcement that the United States would boycott the 1980 Moscow Olympics in protest of the Soviet invasion of Afghanistan. The anti-US sentiment echoes statements made by the Soviet government and by the Soviet-backed government of Afghanistan. © AP Images.

Our government is the only lawful, national and democratic popular government of Afghanistan. We have the support of the broadest sections of the population.

No one can deprive us of our inalienable right to choose our friends nor the right to turn to them for assistance in case of need. We resolutely reject the accusations levelled at the Soviet Union which were contained in the speech. The Soviet Union has rendered us support in our struggle against external aggression in which Washington's participation is no great secret.

Afghanistan Requested Soviet Assistance

In calling upon the Soviet Union for help, we acted in full accordance with Article 51 of the UN Charter, which guarantees us—and any nation which has become the object of aggression—the right to collective self-defence. We also looked for support

Excerpt from US President Jimmy Carter's 1980 State of the Union Address

We superpowers . . . have the responsibility to exercise restraint in the use of our great military force. The integrity and the independence of weaker nations must not be threatened. They must know that in our presence they are secure.

But now the Soviet Union has taken a radical and an aggressive new step. It's using its great military power against a relatively defenseless nation. The implications of the Soviet invasion of Afghanistan could pose the most serious threat to the peace since the Second World War.

The vast majority of nations on Earth have condemned this latest Soviet attempt to extend its colonial domination of others and have demanded the immediate withdrawal of Soviet troops. The Moslem world is especially and justifiably outraged by this aggression against an Islamic people. No action of a world power has ever been so quickly and so overwhelmingly condemned. But verbal condemnation is not enough. The Soviet Union must pay a concrete price for their aggression.

While this invasion continues, we and the other nations of the world cannot conduct business as usual with the Soviet Union. That's why the United States has imposed stiff economic penalties on the Soviet Union. I will not issue any permits for Soviet ships to

to Article 4 of the Soviet Afghan Treaty of Friendship, Good-Neighbourliness and Cooperation.

The Soviet Union, responding to our appeal, fulfilled its treaty obligations and acted in full accordance with international law.

The President of the USA must be perfectly aware that the limited contingent of Soviet troops, introduced into the territory of Afghanistan at our request, is helping us to protect our borders from intrusions from abroad. Relationships between the

fish in the coastal waters of the United States. I've cut Soviet access to high-technology equipment and to agricultural products. I've limited other commerce with the Soviet Union, and I've asked our allies and friends to join with us in restraining their own trade with the Soviets and not to replace our own embargoed items. And I have notified the Olympic Committee that with Soviet invading forces in Afghanistan, neither the American people nor I will support sending an Olympic team to Moscow [for the 1980 Summer Olympic Games.]

The Soviet Union is going to have to answer some basic questions: Will it help promote a more stable international environment in which its own legitimate, peaceful concerns can be pursued? Or will it continue to expand its military power far beyond its genuine security needs, and use that power for colonial conquest? The Soviet Union must realize that its decision to use military force in Afghanistan will be costly to every political and economic relationship it values.

The region which is now threatened by Soviet troops in Afghanistan is of great strategic importance: It contains more than two-thirds of the world's exportable oil. The Soviet effort to dominate Afghanistan has brought Soviet military forces to within 300 miles of the Indian Ocean and close to the Straits of Hormuz, a waterway through which most of the world's oil must flow.

Jimmy Carter, "The State of the Union Address Delivered Before a Joint Session of the Congress: January 23, 1980," The American Presidency Project, www.presidency.ucsb.edu.

Afghan people and the Soviet soldiers are based on sympathy and trust. The Afghan nation makes no claims to the territory of other countries and does not intend to interfere in any other nation's internal affairs.

Afghanistan Is an Independent State
Its [Afghanistan's] territory is not being used for preparations for any attempts to push forward to the Indian Ocean or the Persian

Gulf, the oil-rich zones. All this is a total fabrication. But the chief of the American administration prefers to ignore these perfectly obvious facts. He disregards the assurances expressed both by the Soviet government and by ourselves that as soon as the factors, which prompted us to look to the USSR for help, cease to exist, Soviet units will be withdrawn from Afghanistan.

Isn't it because the President deliberately failed to mention all this that right-wing and imperialist circles within the USA are looking upon events in Afghanistan and the surrounding region as an excuse for undermining detente [the easing of tensions between Communist and democratic nations], and as a basis for the expansionist and imperialist ambitions of the United States itself.

The government and people of the Democratic Republic of Afghanistan resolutely repudiate the interference of the USA in the internal affairs of our country, whatever form it takes— whether as interventionist acts against the Afghan state or provocatory speeches. Afghanistan has been in the past and continues to be an independent and free state.

A Report to the United Nations on the Soviet Atrocities in Afghanistan

Felix Ermacora

Human rights expert Felix Ermacora served as the special rapporteur to the United Nations Commission on Human Rights and as a law professor at the University of Vienna. Ermacora's 1986 report on Soviet atrocities committed in Afghanistan was largely suppressed by the United Nations. Instead of being included in the official UN interim report for that period, it was published as an addendum, which was never translated and thus was not included in documents sent to non-English speaking UN members. The following viewpoint is drawn from a reproduction of Ermacora's report. Ermacora describes numerous atrocities committed in Afghanistan by Soviet or Soviet-controlled military forces, including torture and inhumane treatment of prisoners and brutal attacks on civilians.

New information concerning prison conditions has been communicated to the Special Rapporteur in Quetta by two Australians, Ms. Jenny Lade, teacher of sculpture at the University of Baluchistan [in Pakistan], and Robert Williamson, expert of forestry working on a project financed by the World Bank in Baluchistan, who were kidnapped by members of the

Sassouli tribe on 18 May 1985 while proceeding to the site of the project located in the Maslakh forest reserve (west of Quetta) [the capital of the Pakistani province of Baluchistan]. Detained for two weeks in the tribal area on the border of Pakistan and Afghanistan, they were transferred to Kandahar [in Afghanistan] by a helicopter identified as belonging to the [Soviet-controlled] Afghan military forces. Two days later they were transferred to Kabul and detained in Sadarat Prison. During their transfer from the tribal area to Kandahar and Kabul they were blindfolded and handcuffed. During their detention they were separated.

Life as a Political Prisoner

Detained from 2 June to 27 December 1985 in a cell measuring 10 feet by 10 feet with up to four political prisoners waiting to be convicted (she was told that some of them had been detained for up to 22 months without trial) she was not permitted to inform the Australian Embassy of her detention. The women detained with her were aged between 17 and 65 years and some were accompanied by their babies. During the period of detention, although she received sufficient quantities of food, the nutritional value of the food was so low that she eventually contracted scurvy. Accordingly [sic] to information given to her by an inmate, there had been cases of ill-treatment of women previously detained at the Sadarat Prison (some of them were allegedly hung up by their arms and beaten on their legs, and she had seen an inmate with bruises on her legs). The time outside the cell was limited to half an hour a day. She described the cell as being in poor condition, with a leaking roof and the floor covered with insects and rats. Other inmates could receive parcels once fortnightly from relatives, containing food, clothes and money. However, some of the contents of the parcels were withheld by prison warders.

In October 1985, she was charged with illegal entry into Afghanistan, membership of the CIA and involvement with Pashtu tribesmen for counter-revolutionary activities. Thereafter she was given half an hour to write her defence. During her entire detention she was not allowed either to write to her family or to have a lawyer. However, she was obliged to write two letters in accordance with guidelines, dictated to her by a police officer (interrogator), stating that she was in good health and alive. The letter was sent to the Pakistani authorities and the Australian Embassy in Islamabad. She was released without trial on 27 December 1985, the same day as Mr. Williamson.

Detained for the same period as Ms. Lade, Mr. Williamson was completely isolated from the other detainees for five months. He was not permitted to inform the Australian Embassy or anyone else of his detention. Unlike other inmates, he was not allowed any physical exercise; his only option was to walk up and down his cell. He was charged with illegal entry into Afghanistan, membership of the CIA and involvement with Pashtu tribesmen for counter-revolutionary activities. However, he received enough time and paper to prepare his defence. During his entire detention he was not allowed either to write to his family or to contact a lawyer. He was released without trial on 27 December 1985, the same day as Ms. Lade.

According to information given to him by inmates, there had been cases of torture by electric shocks; he was also told of a 16-year-old detainee and the case of a man kept in detention for three and a half years without trial. Cries and screams could be heard during the night from different parts of the prison. . . .

Torture of Afghan and Pakistani Prisoners

A driver working for the Water and Power Development Authorities project group informed the Special Rapporteur that he had been kidnapped by Asmatullah tribesmen on 29 November 1985 under similar circumstances to those of the two Australians while proceeding to a village located near Chaman. He had also been handed over to Afghan authorities in Spin Baldak and then transferred to a prison in Kandahar. Two and a half months later he was transferred to Pol-i-Charkhi Prison in Kabul, and charged with illegal entry into Afghanistan. According to his testimony,

Pol-i-Charkhi, the largest prison in Afghanistan, is notorious as the site of torture and executions by whichever faction happens to be in power at the time. The building has been attacked many times, and the decades of fighting have left many scars on its exterior. © AP Images/Zaheeruddin Abdullah.

there have been cases of ill-treatment of detainees who were allegedly forced to stand on one leg in the snow for an hour at a time. On 16 August 1986 he was released without trial as part of an exchange of prisoners. It was also stated to the Special Rapporteur that other Pakistani citizens who had been kidnapped under similar circumstances were still in Afghan custody; no further information about the fate of these persons was available.

The Special Rapporteur has been informed about the continuation of torture and ill-treatment in Khad [the Moscow-controlled Afghan secret police] interrogation centres during interrogation. According to new information, during interrogation the following severe methods of torture are still being used on men and women: pulling out finger nails, systematic beating and psychological pressure. Information has been received about particularly harsh disciplinary measures in the Pol-i-Charkhi Prison. Two persons reported that they have been held for days and nights handcuffed and with their knees bound, in a very small, dirty, humid cell. They showed marks on their arms and legs to the Special Rapporteur. One of these persons gave the Special Rapporteur a copy of judgement delivered by a revolutionary court and a copy of a decision releasing the same person in accordance with the implementation of the Amnesty Decree declared on the occasion of the *Loya Jirgah* [a tribal assembly, generally dedicated to resolving disputes] which took place on 4 July 1986. . . .

Taking Children and Training Them as Spies

The Special Rapporteur has received additional information confirming the fact that the educational system in Afghanistan is largely based on non-traditional ideas. This is at variance with article 18, paragraphs 1 and 4, of the International Covenant on Civil and Political Rights. The educational system applied to many children sent abroad through the institution known as *perwarischgahi watan* (homeland nursery) is still in force and children are still enrolled in this institution [for the purpose of Communist indoctrination] against their parents' will. The Special Rapporteur was told that some children are sent to the Soviet Union for a short period of time and used thereafter as spies. A 16-year-old boy informed the Special Rapporteur that he had been sent to the Soviet Union against his will, trained for two months in espionage and forced to collect information on the activities of opposition movements based in Peshawar. . . .

Soviet Soldiers Target Civilians and Their Livelihood

The gravity of the conflict is illustrated by the high civilian casualties resulting from bombardments and massacres which were reported to have occurred during searches for members of opposition movements carried out by the [Soviet and/or Soviet-controlled] military forces. Statistics received by the Special Rapporteur show that the number of civilian deaths has diminished during 1986.

The Special Rapporteur has already provided a statistical survey of civilian casualties during 1985. According to information submitted by the Bibliotheca Afghanica Foundation (Liesthal, Switzerland), civilian casualties from the end of 1985 to September 1986 are of the order of 10,000 to 12,000.

According to statements made by various witnesses to the Special Rapporteur, the governmental forces and/or foreign [Soviet] troops continue to bomb villages, cultivated land and water reservoirs as well as to kill animals in order to deprive the population of their subsistence and force them to leave the rural areas either to seek refuge or to seek shelter in the major cities.

Several witnesses reported on the use by the armed [Soviet] forces of gas, in which a greenish-colored substance was released against members of opposition forces hiding in underground passages or *karez*. The substance reportedly caused serious injuries. The use of chemical weapons has been reported in four instances in Konduz, Paktia, Kabul and Vardak Provinces; the use of napalm and phosphor bombs was reported in four other instances in the provinces of Herat, Paktia and Kabul (twice).

The Special Rapporteur was given information about an incident said to have occurred in mid-August 1986 in the village of Garabad, in Konduz Province, during which [pro-Soviet and/or Soviet-controlled] soldiers first invaded the village in retaliation for an encounter with members of opposition movements and then executed 30 persons, disemboweled a woman with a bayonet and cut off her breasts, and kicked several children to death. Several houses were destroyed and all livestock killed. The witness claimed that he himself had lost 14 family members (three of whom had been killed by bayonets and 11 crushed under the rubble of their house, which had been destroyed by fire).

The Special Rapporteur also learned of several incidents in which reprisals were carried out according to an identical pattern: [Soviet and/or Soviet-controlled] soldiers would retreat after a skirmish, then return to the villages in the vicinity of the

combat zone and enter and search the houses, which they subsequently burned, often killing any survivors with bayonets.

In one particularly horrible incident, several persons had their throats slit with knives. This incident took place in the village of Siyawachan, in Herat Province, in March 1986. Eleven persons were killed, with one survivor currently receiving medical treatment.

More than 100 Cases of Civilian Bombardment Occurred in 1986

Eye-witnesses have informed the Special Rapporteur of civilian deaths during [Soviet] bombing attacks on villages. Some 100 instances of bombardment of civilian targets, or affecting civilian targets were reported during the period under review. According to these witnesses, the bombardments grew particularly intense and numerous after June 1986. Given the large number of incidents, the Special Rapporteur will describe only the following cases, which he believes ought to be brought to the attention of the General Assembly:

- In late March 1986, approximately 350 men, women and children were killed in four villages in the Qarabagh District, Ghazni Province;
- On 12 April 1986, between 800 and 1,000 civilians were killed by soldiers in the Andkhvoy District of Faryab Province during a [Soviet] bombing raid. Several houses were destroyed during this raid. There have also been reports in the same province of 100 civilians killed during encounters on 5 June 1986 between Afghan troops and opposition fighters;
- Following fighting between Afghan troops and members of opposition movements in Kandahar Province in mid-July 1986, approximately 25 civilians were killed.

In addition to the incidents mentioned above, the Special Rapporteur personally saw the bodies of women killed during [Soviet] bombings in Paktia Province.

On a parallel with these incidents, the Special Rapporteur feels compelled to state that a number of civilians are reported to have been killed during attacks by members of opposition movements. The Special Rapporteur was informed that at least 50 civilians and military personnel had been killed and several others wounded in the explosion of a munitions depot on 27 August 1986 at Qargha in Kabul Province. In addition, a bomb explosion at the Jalalabad airport on 11 August 1986 killed approximately 16 persons and wounded several others. Leaders of the [anti-Soviet] opposition movements took credit for both these incidents.

The Intensity of Fighting Makes It Impossible to Assist Injured Civilians

The Special Rapporteur has already had occasion to discuss the humanitarian activities of the International Committee of the Red Cross (ICRC) in his earlier reports. Since then he has noted an increase in the number of civilian casualties and in the severity of injuries, particularly within the last three or four months of this year [1986]. Different sources of information concur that this worsening of the situation is attributable to the intensity of the fighting begun during this period.

According to various sources, ICRC undertook an exploratory mission to assess the prospects for resuming its activities in Afghanistan and to set up a facility that would enable it to resume its humanitarian work.

As stated in earlier reports, the main types of action [by Soviet or Soviet-controlled forces] which have caused deaths and casualties, in particular among the civilian population of Afghanistan, are bombardments, shelling and massacres in reprisal, acts of brutality committed by armed forces, and the use of anti-personnel mines and booby-trap toys. The Special Rapporteur learned that chemical fertilizers, so-called "seism" mines, anti-personnel mines and booby-trap toys were still used. He was also informed of the use of toy-bombs inside houses.

During visits to hospitals at Quetta and Peshawar in September 1986, the Special Rapporteur was able to obtain statistics on civilian casualties. There was a notable increase in the number of wounded since May 1985, peaking in July and August 1986. It was explained to the Special Rapporteur that this aggravation was due to the intensity of fighting which had taken place in Paktia, Paktika, Nangarhar, Herat and Faryab Provinces. For example, in a single hospital, 3,344 patients had been hospitalized between January and July 1986, for either bullet or shrapnel wounds.

Armed Forces Are Using Anti-Personnel Mines and Booby-Trap Toys

The Special Rapporteur has already reported to the General Assembly on the use of anti-personnel mines and booby-trap toys. He was able to see and speak to wounded children whose injuries were caused by the use of these horrible weapons.

In the course of talks held in September 1986, the Special Rapporteur received information which confirmed that the [pro-Soviet] Afghan and/or foreign [i.e., Soviet] armed forces were using anti-personnel mines and booby-trap toys of increasingly varied types.

As regards injuries sustained by children, the Special Rapporteur himself observed that they generally comprise serious leg and hand wounds which frequently result in amputations; this, he was told, was the result of explosions of booby-trap bombs in the form of toys, of anti-personnel mines or of bombardments. The following cases may serve as illustrations:

- A child of two years, hospitalized at Mekka El Mukarramma, at Quetta, is currently undergoing treatment for severe burns sustained on both legs in a fire which totally destroyed his house in July 1985, after a [Soviet] bombing attack on his village, located in Ghazni Province;

- A 17-year-old girl from Ghazni Province had her face completely disfigured by burns in a fire which started when her house was bombed. A piece of shrapnel in her abdomen also injured her entire genital system, for which she is now receiving intensive care. She said that her entire family had been killed during the incident;

- In March 1986, a 13-year-old child from Mazar-e-Sharif in Balkh Province was seriously wounded by exploding knife-like shrapnel. During this incident, which occurred during an aerial bombing, 7 members of his family and 60 other inhabitants of the village perished;

- A 16-year-old boy, a native of Paktika, had his left leg amputated following the explosion of an anti-personnel mine in July 1986.

According to information obtained during the recent visit, [Soviet] booby-trap toys have been distributed along the entire length of the Misamsha-Khost border in the Bangidar Valley, in Paktia Province. . . .

Targeting Afghan Cultural Heritage

The Special Rapporteur has been informed that the Minaret of Herat, the Chesht Mosque and the Herat Great Mosque Jami have been destroyed. These are monuments to which the Convention for the Protection of Cultural Property in the event of Armed Conflict of 14 May 1954 must apply. In response to his letter to the United Nations Educational, Scientific and Cultural Organization requesting additional information, the Special Rapporteur received the following reply on 24 February 1986:

> As part of the international campaign to save the monu-ments of Herat, and at the request of the national authorities, UNESCO dispatched a consultant, Professor Andrea Bruno of Italy, on a mission to Afghanistan from 23 December 1985 to 6 January 1986. The purpose of the mission was to update the campaign plan of action.
>
> Professor Bruno visited only Kabul, where he held tech-nical consultations with the competent authorities in charge of monument preservation. In view of the instructions of the United Nations Security Co-ordinator in New York, no visit to

the Herat region was scheduled, nor did the Kabul authorities propose any such visit. Consequently, Professor Bruno was unable to obtain any on-site information regarding the monuments mentioned in the aforementioned letter.

Apart from the direct consequences of the conflict on the cultural heritage of Afghanistan, the Special Rapporteur has received information indicating a consistent pattern of actions [by Soviet forces] designed to obliterate the evidence of the cultural heritage, mainly through neglect of the side-effects of hostilities. Furthermore, this information shows a deliberate effort to stifle artistic activities and cultural life; museums have suffered, libraries have been destroyed, and artists have been killed or have sought refuge abroad.

Forced Conscription of Men and Children

The Special Rapporteur was informed that, in 1982, the regulations concerning the age for drafting into the [Soviet-controlled Afghan] army had been lowered to 15 years. There was forced conscription and the term of military service rose from two to three years in 1982 and then to four years in 1984.

The Special Rapporteur has learned that such conscription continues, depriving universities and schools of male students. In addition, it would appear that the conscription system is governed by severe discriminatory methods: for example, students from families belonging to the Communist Party or sympathizing with it have the privilege of not joining the army at the age of 15, thus having a chance to continue their studies, at home or abroad. A new feature of conscription has been reported by various reliable persons: political prisoners who have benefited from the amnesty following the commemoration in April 1986 of the Saur Revolution were immediately drafted into the Afghan army. Some of them have served in the militia, where their task has been to pick up young men who are old enough to be conscripted in order to draft them into the army.

Hundreds of Thousands of Afghans Are Driven from Their Homes

As the Special Rapporteur already stated in his previous reports, the instability created by events in Afghanistan since 1979 has led to a massive exodus not only to other countries, particularly Pakistan and the Islamic Republic of Iran, but also from rural areas to the towns.

The situation of internal refugees or displaced persons has not changed since the Special Rapporteur described it in paragraphs 63 to 66 of his previous report to the General Assembly. In addition, the Special Rapporteur has learned that the [Soviet-controlled] Government intends to displace 300,000 persons from the eastern provinces to the south-western provinces. According to information available, most of the population concerned has already sought refuge in Pakistan.

A United Nations Resolution on the Soviet Occupation of Afghanistan

United Nations

In the following viewpoint, the United Nations delivers its second resolution on the state of human rights in Afghanistan. This resolution, adopted in 1986, represents the first time that the UN General Assembly acknowledged the grave humanitarian crisis in Afghanistan under Soviet occupation. The UN would go on to annually re-issue this resolution verbatim until the Soviet Union's voluntary withdrawal from Afghanistan in 1989.

*T*he General Assembly,

Guided by the principles embodied in the Charter of the United Nations, the Universal Declaration of Human Rights, the International Covenants on Human Rights and the humanitarian rules set out in the Geneva Conventions of 12 August 1949,

Aware of its responsibility to promote and encourage respect for human rights and fundamental freedoms for all and resolved to remain vigilant with regard to violations of human rights wherever they occur,

United Nations, "Question of Human Rights and Fundamental Freedoms in Afghanistan," Resolutions Adopted by the General Assembly at its 41st Session, December 4, 1986. Copyright © 1986 by the United Nations. All rights reserved. Reproduced by permission.

Emphasizing the obligation of all Governments to respect and protect human rights and to fulfil the responsibilities they have assumed under various international instruments,

Recalling Commission on Human Rights resolution 1984/55 of 15 March 1984, in which the Commission expressed its concern and anxiety at the continuing presence of foreign [Soviet] forces in Afghanistan, as well as Economic and Social Council resolution 1984/37 of 24 May 1984, in which the Council requested the Chairman of the Commission on Human Rights to appoint a special rapporteur to examine the situation of human rights in Afghanistan,

Recalling also Commission on Human Rights resolution 1985/38 of 13 March 1985, in which the Commission expressed its profound concern at the grave and massive human rights violations in Afghanistan and urged the authorities in that country to put a stop to those violations, in particular the military repression being conducted against the civilian population of Afghanistan,

Recalling further Economic and Social Council decision 1985/147 of 30 May 1985, by which the Council approved the decision of the Commission on Human Rights to extend the mandate of the Special Rapporteur and to request him to report to the General Assembly at its fortieth session and to the Commission at its forty-second session on the situation of human rights in Afghanistan, including the human and material losses resulting from the bombardments of the civilian population,

Recalling resolution 1985/35 of 30 August 1985 of the Sub-Commission on Prevention of Discrimination and Protection of Minorities, in which the Sub-Commission requested the Commission on Human Rights to ask the Special Rapporteur to look into, in particular, the fate of women and children as a consequence of the conflict in Afghanistan,

Recalling also its resolution 40/137 of 13 December 1985, in which it expressed its profound concern that disregard for human rights in Afghanistan was more widespread and that the conflict

Afghan refugees gather in Pakistan in 1980. The UN found that during the 1980s millions of Afghans were forced to leave their homes to escape atrocities and human rights violations. © AP Images/Jeff Robins.

continued to engender human rights violations on a large scale, endangering, as a result, not only the lives of individuals but also the existence of whole groups of persons and tribes,

Taking note of Commission on Human Rights resolution 1986/40 of 12 March 1986 and Economic and Social Council decision 1986/136 of 23 May 1986, by which the Council approved the Commission's decision to extend for one year the mandate of the Special Rapporteur,

Having carefully examined the interim report of the Special Rapporteur on the situation of human rights in Afghanistan, which reveals continuing grave and massive violations of fundamental human rights in that country,

Recognizing that a situation of armed conflict continues to exist in Afghanistan, leaving large numbers of victims without protection or assistance,

Deploring the continuing refusal of the Afghan authorities to co-operate with the Special Rapporteur,

The UN Expresses Concern About Human Rights Violations in Afghanistan

1. *Commends* the Special Rapporteur for his report on the situation of human rights in Afghanistan;

2. *Express once again its deep concern* that the Afghan authorities, with heavy support from foreign troops, are acting with great severity against their opponents and suspected opponents without any respect for the international human rights obligations which they have assumed;

3. *Expresses its grave concern* at the methods of warfare used, which are contrary to international humanitarian standards and the relevant instruments to which the States concerned are parties;

4. *Also expresses its grave concern,* in particular, at the severe consequences for the civilian population of indiscriminate bombardments and military operations primarily targeted on villages and the agricultural structure;

5. *Shares the conviction* of the Special Rapporteur that the prolongation of the conflict increases the seriousness of the gross and systematic violations of human rights already existing in the country;

6. *Expresses once again its profound distress and alarm,* in particular, at the widespread violations of the right to life, liberty and security of person, including the commonplace practice of torture and summary executions of the opponents of the régime, as well as at continuing evidence of a policy of religious intolerance;

7. *Expresses its deep concern* about the number of persons detained for seeking to exercise their human rights and fundamental freedoms, and their detention under conditions contrary to internationally recognized standards;

8. *Notes with great concern* that the educational system does not appear to respect the liberty of parents to ensure the religious

and moral education of their children in conformity with their own convictions;

9. *Notes also with great concern* that such widespread violations of human rights, that have already caused millions of people to flee their homes and country, are still giving rise to large flows of refugees and displaced persons;

10. *Calls once again upon* the parties to the conflict to apply fully the principles and rules of international humanitarian law and to admit international humanitarian organizations, in particular the International Committee of the Red Cross, and to facilitate their operations for the alleviation of the suffering of the people in Afghanistan;

11. *Urges* the authorities in Afghanistan to co-operate with the Commission on Human Rights and its Special Rapporteur, in particular by allowing him to visit Afghanistan;

12. *Requests* the Secretary-General to give all necessary assistance to the Special Rapporteur;

13. *Decides* to keep under consideration, during its forty-second session, the question of human rights and fundamental freedoms in Afghanistan in order to examine this question anew in the light of additional elements provided by the Commission on Human Rights and the Economic and Social Council.

The Rise and Fall of the Taliban in Afghanistan

Kim Masters Evans

Kim Masters Evans is an environmental engineer and educational writer. In the following viewpoint, Evans offers an overview of Afghanistan's long history of internal strife as well as the region's conservative cultural traditions and deeply-held Islamic faith. These factors fostered the rise of the Taliban—an ultraconservative militant political movement—following the 1989 withdrawal of Soviet forces, Evans maintains. She argues that the combination of political instability and fundamentalist religious fervor also led to the alliance of the Taliban and Saudi Arabian terrorist Osama bin Laden. Bin Laden was responsible for several attacks against US interests, culminating with the terror attacks of September 11, 2001, which resulted in the deaths of thousands. Because Afghanistan continued to shield Osama bin Laden following these attacks, the United States invaded the country in October 2001, quickly toppling the Taliban. Osama bin Laden was captured and killed a decade later.

The history of Afghanistan revolves around an ancient group of people called the Pashtun. As described by the article

Kim Masters Evans, "The Wars in Afghanistan and Iraq: Afghanistan," *Information Plus: National Security*, May 2007. Copyright © 2007 Gale, a part of Cengage Learning, Inc. Reproduced by permission. www.cengage.com/permissions.

"Peoples: Pashtun" (*National Geographic*, July 2005), the Pashtun have lived in this region for centuries and survived conquest by many invaders, including the Persians, Macedonians, Turks, and Mongols. They have earned a reputation as being fierce fighters. However, the Pashtun are also known for in-fighting and waging blood feuds among themselves. They are a group of tribes that together make up the largest surviving tribal society in the world. They adhere to an ancient strict code of conduct called *pakhtumwalimale* that specifies rules for all areas of society and everyday life. The Pashtun were known by the Persian term *Afghan* long before their land was called Afghanistan.

A Legacy of War

Afghanistan's Islamic history dates back to the seventh century and is described by the Library of Congress (LOC) in *A Country Study: Afghanistan*. In 637, Muslims from the Arab empire invaded the region and maintained power for several centuries. The LOC notes that "from the seventh through the ninth centuries, most inhabitants of what is present-day Afghanistan, Pakistan, southern parts of the former Soviet Union, and areas of northern India were converted to Sunni Islam."

In *World Factbook: Afghanistan*, the CIA reports that the founding of modern Afghanistan occurred in 1747, when warring Pashtun tribes were united under one leader. At that time the British Empire ruled the land to the east (India and modern-day Pakistan) and the Russians controlled Turkmenistan, Uzbekistan, and Tajikistan to the north. British and Afghan rulers warred over control of Afghanistan until 1919, when the country won its independence. What followed was a series of monarchies that culminated in a 1978 coup, which installed a highly unpopular communist government. In 1979 the Soviet Union invaded Afghanistan to prevent a brewing revolution and preserve communist rule. The Soviets waged a decade-long war but were driven out by well-armed rebels who called themselves the mujahideen (holy warriors).

The Role of Bin Laden in Afghan Affairs

The mujahideen were young Muslims who came from around the world to fight against the Soviet forces as part of a jihad (holy war). In 1980 a wealthy young man named Osama bin Laden traveled from his homeland in Saudi Arabia to help the mujahideen. His role is described at length by the National Commission on Terrorist Attacks upon the United States in *The 9/11 Commission Report* (July 2004). Bin Laden's specialty was raising money and recruiting volunteers, who came to be known as the Arab Afghans. He excelled at organizing fund-raising networks that included charities and wealthy donors throughout the world. These funds were used to buy arms and provide training for the Arab Afghans.

The United States, anxious to see its communist enemy defeated in Afghanistan, supported the mujahideen in its efforts. The *9/11 Commission Report* notes that the United States and Saudi Arabia secretly supplied billions of dollars worth of weapons and equipment to the mujahideen through Pakistani military intelligence. However, there is no record of U.S. involvement with bin Laden or the Arab Afghans, who had their own funding sources. In 1988 the Soviets decided to withdraw from Afghanistan in the face of unrelenting resistance from the mujahideen. Bin Laden and his compatriots were reluctant to dismantle their well-funded and highly trained organization, so they decided to maintain it for future jihads. They began calling it al Qaeda, which means "the base" or "the foundation." In 1991 they set up operations in Sudan at the invitation of that country's leader and maintained camps in Afghanistan and Pakistan to train young militant Muslims as jihadists.

The Taliban Takes Control of Afghanistan

The demise of the communist government in Afghanistan left a power vacuum. Rival mujahideen factions began fighting for control. In *A Country Study: Afghanistan*, the LOC describes these events and notes that during the Soviet occupation the

Osama bin Laden based the bulk of the al Qaeda organization in Afghanistan, where he enjoyed a close relationship with the ruling Taliban. In 1998 he announced his intention to wage jihad against the United States. © AP Images.

mujahideen were often described in the Western press as "'freedom fighters'—as if their goal were to establish a representative democracy in Afghanistan—in reality these groups each had agendas of their own that were often far from democratic." Civil war racked the country until the mid-1990s, when a new political-military force—the Taliban—achieved power. The LOC points out that most members of the Taliban were Pashtun who attended or had recently graduated from religious schools called madrassas in southern Afghanistan and Pakistan.

According to the *9/11 Commission Report*, madrassas are privately funded religious schools that teach strict fundamentalist forms of Islam. Beginning in the 1970s the schools started appearing in southern Pakistan because the government could not afford to educate the many Afghan refugees who had fled there to escape the violence in their own country. The report notes that "these schools produced large numbers of half-educated young men with no marketable skills but with deeply held Islamic views." Eventually, Pakistan became concerned about the presence of so many militant young men within its borders, so it encouraged them to return to Afghanistan and restore order there.

By 1996 the Taliban had seized control over most of Afghanistan. In May of that year bin Laden moved the bulk of his al Qaeda organization from Sudan back to Afghanistan. By this time he had enlarged his focus from regional Islamic causes to what the *9/11 Commission Report* calls "hatred of the United States." This development could be traced back to the 1990 Iraqi invasion of Kuwait. At that time bin Laden reportedly approached Saudi rulers and offered to organize a mujahideen force to drive out the Iraqis, but he was turned down. Saudi Arabia allied with the United States during the subsequent Persian Gulf War (1990–1991) and allowed U.S. troops to deploy from Saudi soil. This decision infuriated Islamic fundamentalists because they opposed the presence of nonbelievers in Saudi Arabia, the birthplace of Muhammad (c. 570–632). After criticizing Saudi leaders, bin Laden had his passport taken away. However, he managed to leave the country in 1991 and eventually turned up in Afghanistan, where he developed a close relationship with the Taliban leader Mohammed Omar (1961–).

Throughout the remainder of the decade bin Laden expanded his al Qaeda network with the blessing of the Afghan Taliban regime. In 1998 he publicly announced his intention to wage a jihad against the United States by issuing a fatwa (an interpretation of Islamic law usually written by a scholar or religious authority) that was published in an Arabic-language newspaper in London. . . . Al Qaeda operatives then carried out a series of attacks against U.S. interests, including the 1998 bombings at two U.S. embassies in Africa, the 2000 bombing of the USS *Cole* in Yemen, and 9/11. . . .

The Abusive Rule of the Taliban

Peter L. Bergen claims in *Holy War, Inc.: Inside the Secret World of Osama bin Laden* (2001) that the U.S. government was optimistic about the Taliban when it first seized power in Afghanistan. Bergen writes, "The State Department, which relied heavily on the Pakistanis for information on Afghanistan, was willing to embrace any group that looked as if it might bring some degree of stability to the country." Besides security concerns, the U.S. government had other priorities in Afghanistan, including a planned oil pipeline by a U.S. energy company and curbing Afghanistan's enormous illegal drug trade. There was hope that the new Afghan regime could help in these areas. However, U.S. leaders quickly became disillusioned with the Taliban.

Bergen notes that the Taliban imposed laws blending "ultra-purist" Islam with traditional Pashtun customs. The result was a society in which men were forbidden to shave or trim their beards. All forms of entertainment, such as listening to the radio or flying a kite, were outlawed. Women were forced to cover themselves with thick head-to-toe cloaks called burkas and were not allowed in public unless accompanied by a male relative. Most women were forbidden to work or obtain an education. Taliban laws were enforced by religious police who roamed the streets, beating violators with sticks. By this time the Afghan people had suffered from decades of war that had destroyed most of the country's infrastructure; their economy was in shambles and food was in short supply.

As 2001 began, the United States was well aware that the Taliban was harboring terrorists. In 1999 and 2000 the United Nations (UN) Security Council had imposed economic sanctions on Afghanistan for a variety of infractions, including providing sanctuary to and training international terrorists, particularly bin Laden and his associates. In December 2000 the UN demanded that bin Laden be surrendered and that all terrorist training camps be closed within a month. The Taliban angrily refused to comply, insisting that there was no evidence against bin Laden and that the sanctions were motivated by anti-Islamic sentiment.

The United States Invades Afghanistan and Topples the Taliban

Within days after 9/11, the United States had decided to target Afghanistan. In an address to Congress on September 20, 2001, President [George W.] Bush publicly blamed al Qaeda and bin Laden for the attacks and demanded that the Taliban hand over bin Laden and his top lieutenants or the United States would strike. According to the *9/11 Commission Report*, the demands had already been privately passed to the Taliban through the Pakistani government, which the United States had warned "would be at risk" unless it helped the United States against Afghanistan. As expected, Afghanistan refused to comply with U.S. demands.

By October 2001 a U.S. war plan had been compiled that was originally called Infinite Justice. However, fears about offending religious sensibilities prompted a quick name change to Operation Enduring Freedom (OEF) when U.S. officials learned that Muslims associate the term *infinite justice* with God's power. The *9/11 Commission Report* indicates that OEF had four phases:

- Phase one—deploy U.S. forces to Afghanistan's neighbors in readiness for an invasion. This step was begun almost immediately and entailed the cooperation of Pakistan and Uzbekistan.

- Phase two—conduct air strikes on Afghan targets and pair Special Operations teams with Taliban opposition groups to conduct damaging raids on al Qaeda strongholds. Even before this time, the CIA had been collaborating with opposition groups in northern Afghanistan known collectively as the Northern Alliance. Phase two began on October 7, 2001, and proceeded quickly with the help of United Kingdom (UK) military forces. By the end of the month most of the phase 2 objectives had been achieved.

- Phase three—launch a ground invasion of Afghanistan to "topple the Taliban regime and eliminate al Qaeda's sanctuary." By early December 2001 the coalition of U.S. and Northern Alliance forces, with the assistance of UK special forces, had captured all major Afghan cities. However, bin Laden and Omar escaped.

- Phase four—the United States called this phase "security and stability operations." It began on December 22, 2001, when Hamid Karzai (1957–; an Afghani Pashtun) was installed as the head of the nation's interim government.

Afghanistan's Current System of Government

Following the U.S. invasion, Afghanistan began a series of democratic reforms. In 2004 the first national presidential election put Karzai in power for a five-year term. Even though the election itself was relatively violence-free, the country continued to struggle with internal problems. In 2009 Karzai was reelected amid widespread allegations of voter fraud and intimidation. Nick Schifrin reports in "With All Polling Stations Counted, Karzai Has 54% of Afghan Vote" (ABCNews.com, September 16, 2009) that Western observers suggested that 1 million to 1.5 million votes were fraudulent, representing one quarter of all the votes cast. In addition, Schifrin notes that much of Afghanistan was under Taliban control at the time of the election. Taliban leaders reportedly threatened attacks against voters and prevented people from voting as much as possible.

CHAPTER 2

Issues and Controversies
Surrounding Afghanistan

Chapter Exercises

1. Analyze the Cartoon

Question 1: What do the snake charmer and snake represent?

Question 2: What do the two lumps in the snake's body represent? What is the artist suggesting will happen to the snake charmer?

Question 3: What is the artist saying about the fate of US forces in Afghanistan? Do you agree or disagree? Why or why not?

2. Writing Prompt

Assume the role of an activist and write a newspaper editorial aimed at drawing attention to the plight of women and girls in Afghanistan during the Soviet occupation, under Taliban rule, or following the US invasion.

3. Group Activity

Break into groups and debate the use of land mines and "total warfare" by Soviet forces in Afghanistan. Was it justified? Did the use of indiscriminate, overwhelming military force by the Soviets justify the extreme measures taken by mujahideen fighters? Was US covert military support of these groups justified?

Genocide Was an Accepted Soviet Anti-Guerilla Tactic

Claude Malhuret

Claude Malhuret is a former executive director of the international medical humanitarian organization Doctors Without Borders. He has also served as France's Secretary of State for Human Rights and is currently the mayor of Vichy, France. In the following viewpoint, Malhuret details atrocities committed by Soviet troops in Afghanistan, witnessed firsthand by doctors. Malhuret asserts that doctors witnessed the deliberate bombing of hospitals, wanton destruction of entire civilian villages, and the excessive use of land mines and booby traps targeting agricultural infrastructure and children. In 1983 Malhuret predicted that the Soviet Union—with its superior military technology and vast funding—would ultimately overpower the Afghan resistance, even if it took several decades. Little could Malhuret have predicted that the Soviets would voluntarily withdraw from Afghanistan just six years later.

For three years now, Médecins sans Frontières [MSF]—Doctors Without Borders—has been in Afghanistan. The first medical teams it sent arrived in May 1980, five months after the Soviet invasion. Since then, we have sent 162 physicians

Claude Malhuret, "Report from Afghanistan," *Foreign Affairs*, Winter 1983–1984. Reprinted by permission of Foreign Affairs. Copyright © 1984 by the Council on Foreign Relations, Inc. www.ForeignAffairs.com.

and nurses who replace each other in relays for periods of four to eight months, providing an uninterrupted MSF presence. We have equipped and operated a total of 12 hospitals in the provinces of Nuristan, Paktia, Badakhshan (close to the Soviet border), Wardak (some 40 km from Kabul), Bamiyan, Uruzgan, and Zabul. Four of these hospitals were deliberately bombed and destroyed by Soviet planes in the fall of 1981. We evacuated two other hospitals in areas where we felt the need for medical services was limited and where local medics whom we have trained have been able to take over. At the present time [1983], the MSF has 22 persons working in six hospitals. From our uninterrupted presence in Afghanistan, we have been able to evaluate the situation in the country since the beginning of the war, specifically in the areas where we are working. The current situation in Afghanistan is one of protracted war. The duration and character of the war derive directly from the Soviet style of anti-guerrilla warfare.

A Policy of Attacking the Civilian Population
Guerrilla warfare has already demonstrated its effectiveness elsewhere, and until recently no one has known how to counter it. The scattering of populations, the creation of village strongholds, and control and card-indexing of inhabitants have proved to be very useful means of restricting guerrilla advances, but the resistance fighters have always won out in the end.

It is true that there are examples to the contrary, such as the victory of the British army in Malaysia, and that of the French expeditionary corps in Algeria. But in the latter case, de Gaulle realized that France's long-term position was untenable and so he complied with the demands of the National Liberation Front [of Algeria], even though the Front was in a very poor military position when negotiations began.

Totalitarian regimes have analyzed these repeated failures and found a new answer to the guerrilla "problem," one that is simple, logical and effective. Since the basis of the strength of a resistance movement lies in the practice that Mao Zedong called "the fish taking to the water," the easiest way to separate the guerrillas from the population is to empty the fish bowl and capture its contents. In other words, an effective counter-strategy in the face of guerrilla action involves massive reprisals against the population, sometimes including the extermination of a large part of that population.

Exterminating Populations Is an Increasingly Popular Anti-Insurgent War Tactic

Some might think that such prospects would be repulsive to even the most determined invader. But this has not been the case; this philosophy has become a reality before our very eyes over the past several years. In the province of Ogaden, which revolted against the regime in power in Ethiopia, towns and villages were leveled one after the other. Nearly one million refugees—almost all the inhabitants—are now in refugee camps in nearby Somalia. And air units from Addis Ababa have no scruples about making raids on the camps.

In Kampuchea [Cambodia], the Vietnamese victory over the Khmer Rouge four years ago would never have been possible if the people had not been starved into submission by the Vietnamese, who feared that part of the relief support might fall to the enemy forces of Pol Pot. While tens of thousands of Kampucheans died of hunger and hundreds of thousands fled into Thailand, thousands of tons of food provided by international relief organizations spoiled on the docks of Kompong Som. The only portions of these supplies that were used went to feed the occupying Vietnamese forces and the Kampucheans under control in the pacified areas.

This type of warfare is currently being used in Afghanistan, the only difference being that the Afghan resistance groups have thus far made it fail. It may therefore be more difficult to recognize the pattern in all of these anti-guerrilla campaigns, but their common characteristics can be divided into three main categories: how the Soviet version of anti-guerrilla warfare compares with traditional Western anti-guerrilla warfare; what specific means it uses; and what the final outcome is.

Traditional Anti-Insurgency vs. Soviet-Style Anti-Insurgency

One difference between the type of warfare used by the Russians in Afghanistan and that used by Western armies, such as the French in Algeria or the Americans in Vietnam, is that Western armies try to control the population and make every effort to prevent infiltration by guerrillas. From the bases they set up in towns, they try to establish a sphere of influence, to find support in the villages and hamlets, and to create militias to defend areas that might be attacked by guerrilla fighters before reinforcements from the regular army arrive. To ensure that resistance groups cannot get supplies from the people, the Western armies set up protected villages where the people are brought together and where food, supplies, and livestock are stored.

Manhunts are continuously organized, from the bases that are considered safe, to capture or kill guerrillas or to seize their caches of arms and ammunition. In all, despite the irresponsible acts committed by the French army in Algeria and the U.S. Army in Vietnam, their anti-guerrilla warfare was based on one principle: to obtain the support of the population by any means, such as by giving privileges to newfound allies and by waging a hard war against the *enemy*. I have already noted the poor results of this type of warfare.

The Soviets operate differently. In Afghanistan, the towns held by the occupying Soviet forces are not used as bases to secure a hold over the neighboring areas. The towns are used as garrisons and as logistical stepping-stones. They provide storage facilities, aviation bases, barracks, and strongholds. The rest of the country is not under Soviet control. Protected villages do not exist. No effort is made to offer privileges to try to win over the population. The few military operations that

Estimated Afghan Casualties During the Soviet Occupation

Mujahideen
    Killed: 75,000–90,000
    Wounded: more than 75,000

Civilians
    Killed: 600,000–2,000,000
    Wounded: nearly 3 million

Refugees
    Driven out of Afghanistan: 5 million
    Internally displaced: 2 million

Total killed, wounded, or displaced
    10,750,000–12,165,000

Total population
    1979 (last official census): 15,551,358
    2012 (estimate): 30,419,928

involve ground forces are merely for strategic purposes. Some examples are the engagements that have taken place on the road from Kabul to the Soviet border, in the Panjshir Valley and the Wakhan corridor; operations there are not designed to capture resistance fighters.

The reason for this difference in anti-guerrilla tactics is very simple: the Soviets are not as naïve as the Westerners. They understood long ago—perhaps back at the time of the 1933 Ukrainian genocide when this tactic was used quite successfully—that a war involving guerrillas and anti-guerrilla fighters would never be won by either side if the emphasis was placed on being in the good graces of the population. On the contrary, the war would be won by the side that succeeded in making terror reign.

Soviets Used Overwhelming Ground Forces Against Civilians

This brings me to the second aspect: specific means used to counter resistance movements. This does not involve a warm bath/cold shower tactic, but the exclusive use of boiling water—again and again and again, until both the guerrilla fighters and the population ask for mercy.

During the first phase, until late 1980, air and ground equipment and infantry units were brought together to establish the reign of terror in this fashion. To mention just one example, in the province of Hazarajat in central Afghanistan, several hundred armored vehicles would leave either Kabul or Jaghori and occupy a valley that could easily be entered. The population, which had warning either by rumor or because they had seen the helicopter movement, fled into the mountains. The Soviet troops therefore entered empty villages where they remained for a few days, harassed by the Muslim resistance groups—the Mujahedeen—who also barred their access to the upper valleys. During those few days, the soldiers pillaged and burned homes, set fire to crops and dragged off with them the few inhabitants left behind—mostly old people, whom they interrogated or summarily executed.

The Scorched Earth Campaign

In 1980, three of these raids by Soviet troops took place along the Shibar Pass road; the soldiers thereby managed to occupy Bamiyan, Yakaolang, and Panjau for about ten days in June with 300 armored vehicles, in August (again with 300 armored vehicles), and in September (with 120 armored vehicles). In their last attack, the Russians destroyed everything in sight, set fire to crops, and burned bazaars to the ground in Panjau, Yakaolang, and several villages on the road to Shibar. They left the former American hospital in Yakaolang in ruins.

During a similar expedition in the fall of 1980, many homes were burned down in the region of Turkmen, west of Kabul, and the small hospital in Lolenj was also completely destroyed. The same kinds of destruction took place in mid-December in the northern part of Ghazni province. When one of our medical teams arrived two days after the end of the fighting, fires were still smoldering in a number of villages, and people were being wounded by booby traps left behind by the Soviet troops. Once again, the effect sought was terror, not strictly military victory.

Since late 1980, warfare using such operations has dropped off, probably because the Red Army has lost too many of its troops. But the Russians have now found other ways to impose a reign of terror, particularly by the use of air raids against which the poorly equipped resistance fighters are completely defenseless. In the Hazarajat region, for example, the villages bombed in the last two years are much too numerous to be listed here in full. Just a few of the targets were Jaghori, Panjau, Behsud, Jalrez and Waras. In Jalrez, a home where a wedding was taking place was bombed and the tragedy left several dozen victims. In Waras, where the independent provisional government of Hazarajat has its headquarters, the helicopters bypassed this organization, which should have been a tempting target, and attacked the village bazaar.

Soviet Forces Extensively Use Land Mines and Booby-Trapped Toys

Military intervention carried out mainly by helicopter also includes dropping mines and booby-trapped toys. I shall not go into detail, but only stress two points. First, camouflaged anti-personnel mines are not designed to kill, but to injure. The Russians know quite well that in this type of war, an injured person is much more trouble than a dead person. The injured person demobilizes fighters who have to transport him, and, of course, he can no longer fight. In many cases, he will die several days or weeks later from gangrene or from staphylococcus or gram-negative septicemia, with atrocious suffering, which further depresses those who must watch him die. The MSF has also seen the damage caused by the explosion of booby-trapped toys, in most cases plastic pens or small red trucks, which are choice terror weapons. Their main targets are children whose hands and arms are blown off. It is impossible to imagine any objective that is more removed from conventional military strategy, which forswears civilian targets.

The second aim of dropping of anti-personnel mines is to affect the economy. First, troops try to set up a blockade using mines that are scattered by the thousands along the passes leading to Pakistan (but with almost no success), and second, they try to scatter the people's livestock. When I arrived in Afghanistan for the first time in 1980, I was immediately struck by the number of goats and cows that had legs in splints made of bamboo sticks and tied with wire. The herdsmen explained to me what had happened: these animals had stepped on mines and been injured as a result of the explosion. But the greatest loss, the herdsmen told me, is not so much the ones with splints, but rather all those animals that were killed from secondary infections. And although the Afghans clear the mines from the roads to prevent more human deaths, the animals in the fields continue to get killed. Livestock in several regions of the country have been slaughtered in this way. The effect of this slaughtering on the food supply in Afghanistan is clear.

Using Refugees as Part of a Military Strategy

Another point to be considered is the question of refugees—those still in Afghanistan as well as those who have fled. These refugees should not be considered in the traditional way, as an unfortunate but unintended consequence of the war, but rather as part of Soviet warfare strategy, the same that was used in Kampuchea, the Ogaden and Eritrea. The objective is, as mentioned earlier, to evacuate the country in order to isolate the guerrilla fighters.

The methodical pursuit of this objective is the only possible explanation for the incredible number of Afghan refugees. Some flee the country to Iran and Pakistan, where they are once again "used" by the Russians, whose agents infiltrate the refugees' ranks to further aggravate the conflicts that exist in Pakistan between different ethnic groups, as many believe is happening in Baluchistan. The figures for Afghan refugees in Pakistan and Iran as reported to international bodies run in excess of 4 million. Out of an Afghan population of 15 to 17 million, this figure is already enormous.

But to this figure must be added the hundreds of thousands of "internal" refugees who remain within Afghanistan. They have fled to the main towns, where they come under the control of the state army. Thus, this enlarged refugee count should be compared not to the total population of Afghanistan, but to the population in the rural areas that are held by the resistance fighters. When one adds to that the number of persons killed either in the fighting or by diseases that frequently find their cause in malnutrition—especially among children—one can better understand why that Soviet strategy is highly effective and that it has no doubt been responsible for chasing nearly half of the population away from guerrilla strongholds.

Also, several thousand children are sent to the Soviet Union to study to be officers one day in the Socialist Republic of Afghanistan; this offers a very close comparison with the Russians' "liberation" of the southern republics of the U.S.S.R. in the 1920s and 1930s, which led to a total victory over what has been called the Basmachi ("bandit") revolt.

The Soviet Union Has Targeted Doctors Without Borders

Before coming to the last issue, which concerns the final outcome of the tactics just discussed, a word must be said about one of the conditions needed for this strategy to be a success: secrecy.

International public opinion would never accept such enormities if it were informed daily on the developments in Afghanistan. The need for secrecy explains why borders are systematically closed and why journalists are not allowed to enter the country. Of course, some journalists disregard this, but they

Bernard Kouchner, a physician with Doctors Without Borders, examines an Afghan patient in Wardak province in 1984. Doctors with the organization witnessed firsthand the atrocities committed by the Soviet army against the Afghans. ©Jose Nicolas/Sygma/Corbis.

are so few in number that their reports draw little attention. Compare, for instance, the amount of coverage on Afghanistan with that given for several years on the war in Vietnam.

The French physicians who have been on permanent duty in Afghanistan for the last four years have become key eyewitnesses, and in spite of their lack of experience in journalism, they have been able to make up somewhat for the negligence of news reporting. I use the word "negligence" because, if a small organization like ours can succeed in maintaining more than 20 physicians on permanent duty in four provinces in Afghanistan, despite government acts of violence against them, the news media could do likewise. The Russians cannot tolerate the fact that we are there to witness what is happening, and we have therefore become their target. In 1980 and 1981, four MSF hospitals were deliberately destroyed by MI-24 helicopters. Two other hospitals in the region of Panjshir, which are operated by another French organization, Aide Medicale Internationale, were destroyed in the same way. May I add that one of the hospitals had a big red cross clearly visible on its roof.

Also, on several occasions, the physicians themselves have been pursued by Soviet soldiers who had in their possession photos of the doctors that they showed to the people they questioned. All the doctors have managed to get away except one, Dr. Philippe Augoyard, who was captured in January 1983. But we do not think that the Russians will try that type of operation again, as it proved disastrous for their image in Europe—especially of course in France. Rather than discouraging new recruits, which was probably the goal, the Augoyard case let physicians in other countries know about our work. Such incidents result in a bad press that affects the Soviets in other spheres. At the present time, only 50 percent of our medical teams are French; the remainder are Dutch, English, Belgian, Swiss, Scandinavian, and other nationalities. If, for example, a Dutch doctor were arrested in Afghanistan, the anti-Soviet publicity would certainly influence the ongoing debate over the installation of American missiles in Europe.

Despite These Tactics, the Soviets Cannot Gain a Foothold

Now we come to the question of the final outcome of the Soviet strategy. The examples given above concerned Kampuchea and Ethiopia. The reason for this is that Afghanistan is not a very good example to illustrate Soviet anti-guerrilla warfare, precisely because the results have so far been unsuccessful. The towns of Afghanistan, the main bases for Soviet intervention, are poorly controlled. Not a week goes by without word of an attack against the government or against communist-bloc embassies in Kabul. In response, the heavily commercial districts in big cities such as Herat and Kandahar were reportedly severely bombed and nearly destroyed by planes because they had gone over to the resistance—just another example of the Soviet terror strategy and massive destruction, which can be contrasted with the house-by-house taking of the Algiers Casbah by the French army in 1970, with little loss to property or human life. The Soviet strongholds of Bamiyan, Ghazni, Gardez, and Khost are completely encircled by the Mujahedeen. In Bamiyan, for example, a garrison composed of 200 Russians and 200 Afghans has its post high up on a peak; supplies reach the garrison by helicopter. Helicopters are therefore gaining in importance for the Soviets as a means of transport between towns because communication links are not at all under control, although efforts have recently been made to improve them.

The puppet government of President Babrak Karmal has also attempted psychological warfare, by trying to play on local antagonisms among the Pushtun tribes. But the government has not been very successful at this, particularly since the death in 1981 of Faiz Mohammed, Minister for Tribal Affairs, who was killed by a group he was trying to bribe.

The cease-fire agreements that have been made have worked as much in favor of the resistance fighters as they have in favor of the government leaders, and they are based more on a balance of power than on a successful psychological warfare strategy. . . .

The Mujahedeen Are Not Cowed

The number of armored vehicles that have been destroyed by resistance forces is incredibly large, considering their outdated weaponry and suicidal tactics (such as leaping onto tanks with homemade gasoline bombs). We counted more than 600 vehicles destroyed in the areas where we work, which, when extrapolated, comes to a total figure of some three to four thousand for the entire country. This figure is generally found to be so unbelievable that, whenever I mention it, I never fail to have with me a set of slides to document what I am saying.

The economic blockade has also not succeeded. The border areas are as easily accessible as they were before it was imposed; our medical teams need only three days to reach the central province of Hazarajat. Our movement is not restricted, as people generally think; we travel by car or truck, and only during the day.

Setting fire to crops and storage shelters is another anti-guerrilla tactic, but its effect is limited because less than half the amount of food that was needed before the war is needed now due to the diminished population. In addition, caravans going to and from Pakistan continue to bring fresh produce. Another striking—and ironic—example of the ambiguous effect on the economy, also from Hazarajat, is the need in Kabul for firewood, which has forced the government to deal with the resistance. The resistance fighters bring wood to government outposts and exchange it for salt or sugar from Kabul.

Despite the attempts to restrict the food supply, trends in local market prices indicate that the blockade is not working. Some prices have actually dropped since the Soviet invasion. . . .

No End in Sight

The examples illustrating the poor short-term effect of Soviet strategy suggest a rather optimistic trend with regard to the Afghan resistance movement, but my conclusion is much less so. Everything I have said about the current situation shows that the war in Afghanistan is one in which the balance of power has not changed in four years, in spite of the fact that the two adversaries are unequally matched—on one side the world's biggest army, on the other a handful of people standing tall against the invader. There is no sign of any change soon in this state of affairs, and I do not believe that the Afghans can be beaten in the short or medium term. But Soviet strategy involves two aspects that may make the outcome in Afghanistan differ from the Western experience; one, already mentioned, is the use of mass terror, completely unlike any of the more moderate types of intervention. The second is that the Soviets can afford a protracted war in the short term for the sake of a long-term victory.

The Russians do not need smashing victories to announce to their citizenry, as Soviet public opinion does not influence Soviet policy. Catastrophes, such as that in the Salang tunnel where several hundred Soviet and communist-regime troops (and civilians) were killed, do not incite an outcry in Moscow for Soviet "boys" to come home. The Soviet army can wait it out as long as it did for the Basmachi revolt to end—and it waited for that for 20 years. It can wait even longer if necessary. The Afghan resistance will hold out for a long time, but in the end it will probably be beaten. It might not be beaten, however, if in the coming years there is a profound change in the international balance of power and in the reactions of Westerners to Soviet totalitarianism. It is not impossible that this change could take place, but only a very wise person would dare to predict the future of Afghanistan.

VIEWPOINT 2

Soviet Land Mines Endangered Children but Did Not Specifically Target Them

Rae McGrath

Rae McGrath served in the British Army for eighteen years as a military engineer—a role that often includes deploying land mines. He used this expertise and founded the Mines Advisory Group, a nonprofit organization that works with local communities to clear land mines and unexploded ordnance in war-torn regions. In the following viewpoint, McGrath maintains that Soviet mines were produced in the millions and deployed extensively in Afghanistan. The author asserts that reports show the Soviet army crafted mines that resembled toys, deliberately targeting children. McGrath argues, however, that although Soviet mines caused tremendous harm, especially to children, they were not purposely made to look like toys.

Children ... face the greatest risk [from land mines], primarily because of their restricted vision of the ground ahead. Children are also most likely to be distracted by objects or activity at the periphery of their vision; they may spend comparatively long periods actually looking in a different direction to that in which they are moving and, of course, children may run for long

Rae McGrath, "Vulnerability and Avoidance," *Landmines: Legacy of Conflict: A Manual for Development Workers.* Oxford, UK: Oxfam, 1994. Copyright © 1994 by Rae McGrath and Mines Advisory Group. All rights reserved. Reproduced by permission.

periods and change direction frequently, for no particular reason, without prior observation of the ground ahead. The height of a child is critical and may mean that a mine, which is clearly visible from several feet away to an adult, is actually impossible for the child to see until it is almost underfoot, particularly if the mine is surrounded by well-grown vegetation.

Soviet Land Mines Were Not Designed to Target Children

It should first be emphasised that there is no evidence and no probability that anti-personnel mines have ever been purposely manufactured to look like toys or other everyday objects. This has become a common rumour in war-affected regions and may be used as deliberate propaganda, as was the case in Afghanistan, where it was an oft-repeated accusation against Soviet forces. In some instances such rumours have been, carelessly or irresponsibly, given credence by aid workers. The danger of this type of rumour is the confusion and fear naturally raised within the

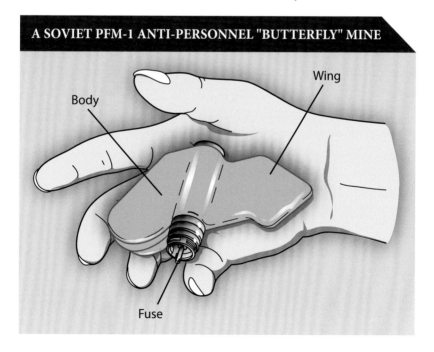

A SOVIET PFM-1 ANTI-PERSONNEL "BUTTERFLY" MINE

Wing

Body

Fuse

community, particularly among returning refugees. There is also a potentially negative impact on the collation of reliable data relating to mine dissemination. Although there is no indication that anti-personnel mines have been deliberately made in the shape of toys or other everyday objects, there is some evidence that individual soldiers, and possibly units, have booby-trapped children's toys and household objects, but nothing to suggest that these actions have been initiated or even supported at a higher military or political level.

Having excluded the likelihood of purpose-manufactured devices which resemble toys, it must be said that some mines, because of their appearance, may have a particular attraction for children. The Soviet PFM-1 "butterfly" mine, sown in massive numbers in Afghanistan, has none of the physical characteristics normally associated with a mine and may clearly attract attention from children. (There are technical design reasons for the shape of the PFM-1: the thick wing contains the liquid explosive and the thin wing ensures that the mine glides after release from its container to obtain a wide area of coverage from each batch of mines.) The unusual appearance of anti-personnel devices like the Italian VS-69 Valmara, a lethal bounding fragmentation mine, certainly arouses the curiosity of children until they are made aware of the deadly nature of the mine. Its danger is increased because, since it is both tripwire-initiated and a direct-pressure device, a curious child may be killed without actually touching the mine itself.

Children Use Mines as Toys

However, the most insidious threat arises from the inventive nature of children and their ability, particularly in poor communities, to put the most mundane and unlikely objects to good use for their entertainment. This is a global phenomenon well-illustrated even in the UK and Ireland and the US, where children used to make carts out of orange boxes and pram wheels. In regions where mines have been widely disseminated they be-

Young Afghan children look for scrap metal and shrapnel from land mines in fields outside their village in 2012. The area was heavily mined during the Soviet invasion of Afghanistan two decades earlier. © Javier Manzano/The Washington Post/Getty Images.

come a familiar sight to children, and a casual attitude to mines is often encouraged by the irresponsible behaviour of soldiers and other adults, who may disarm mines and leave them carelessly on view or even allow children to handle them. The results are well illustrated by [a] photograph . . . of a little boy in Iraqi Kurdistan proudly playing with his home-made truck—the rear wheels made from VS-50 anti-personnel mines with a nail driven through them to form the axle.

Adult Attitudes Put Children at Risk

This lack of sensible respect for mines may be partly a result of children's naturally adventurous and careless nature—but a contributory factor is undoubtedly the attitude of adults, often the child's own parents, who themselves often pay little regard to the danger of mines and may even disarm them and keep them in and around their houses.

As a visitor to many aid agency offices in mined countries, the author could add the observation that field staff who use disarmed fragmentation mines as paper-weights are hardly encouraging a realistic respect for the danger of mines among the community in which they work. "Practice what you preach" should certainly be the rule, particularly among agencies who work closely with children.

Soviets Used Chemical Weapons Against Afghan Mujahideen and Civilians

Stuart J.D. Schwartzstein

Stuart J.D. Schwartzstein has worked in foreign affairs since the 1970s. He has served in the US State Department, the US Department of Defense, the Center for Strategic and International Studies, and in the Coalition Provisional Authority in Baghdad (Iraq). In the following viewpoint, Schwartzstein maintains that Soviet forces used chemical weapons against Afghan insurgents and civilians, both to cause battlefield casualties and to terrorize non-combatant civilian populations. Schwartzstein argues that Soviet forces used Afghanistan as a test bed for new chemical weapons. Use of such weapons was a violation of international law. Although Schwartzstein's report was widely published, it failed to inspire any sort of coordinated international action to curb Soviet aggression or prevent atrocities in Afghanistan.

If there is no doubt that the invasion and occupation of Afghanistan by Soviet forces is a brutal act violating norms of civilized conduct among nations—and indeed, most nations of the world have condemned the Soviet Union for this—equally worthy of strong condemnation are the means by which the Soviet military is attempting to impose its will on an independent people. There is no scarcity of accounts of brutality, of destruction on a large scale, of massacres of noncombatants (women, children, and old men), of destruction of food crops, torture, rape, pillage—in short, the savaging of a country and its people. But the use of one particular category of weaponry by the Soviets in Afghanistan merits special consideration: the use of chemical and toxin weapons [Toxin weapons may be derived from biological agents, although they are themselves chemical. Chemical weapons are governed by the 1925 Geneva Protocol prohibiting their *use*, while toxin weapons are governed by the 1972 Biological and Toxin Weapons Convention prohibiting their *production*. The Soviet Union is signatory to both.]. Their use not only has enormous implications, but should be viewed internationally as an important humanitarian issue.

There can be no doubt now that chemical weapons, including the newly discovered mycotoxins [toxins derived from fungi], are being used in Afghanistan by the Soviets (as they are being used by Soviet surrogates in Southeast Asia). If there remain many questions to be answered about details of use and of agents used—and there are—the basic fact that the Soviets have resorted to such weapons is now, tragically, incontrovertible.

Evidence for Soviet Use of Chemical Weapons in Afghanistan

The charges of Soviet use of such illegal weapons have not been made lightly, nor have they been made without abundant evidence. Evidence available includes:

1. testimony of eyewitnesses to attacks (including freedom fighters, journalists, and noncombatant refugees);
2. testimony of those who have seen and treated—or attempted to treat—victims of attacks (including physicians and refugee workers);
3. testimony of Soviet and Kabul-regime defectors;

4. analysis of physical samples;
5. photographic evidence—of an attack and of physical effects of exposure to chemical (or toxin) weapons.

There are, literally, hundreds of eyewitness accounts of chemical attacks by Soviet forces. Even if we accept the likelihood that not all accounts are accurate or true—and for any sort of phenomenon that is likely to be the case—we are still left with an overwhelming mass of testimony. That testimony is further strengthened by the fact that for most Afghan *mujahidin* the use of chemical weapons is only a minor element in the continued fight against the massive and technologically superior Soviet forces. (Much of the testimony that has been collected has not come easily, but has emerged only after questioning—questions, for example, of how certain injuries were sustained.) Yet, some reports have no doubt gained currency because of the bizarre effects that some of the chemical weapons have had.

Evaluating Eyewitness Testimony from Victims

The testimony of Afghan eyewitnesses has been supplemented by that of journalists. Most importantly, a Dutch journalist, Bernd de Bruin, was not only an eyewitness to an attack in 1981, but filmed it—and himself sustained injuries as a result of exposure to chemical agents.

In considering eyewitness testimony, two important things should be borne in mind: 1) that, given the remote areas in which most of the attacks take place, the difficult terrain that any survivors must cross to reach the outside world, and the likelihood that in many cases there are no survivors, any eyewitness testimony at all is remarkable; and 2) that given the determination of the Afghan resistance fighters to continue to fight, relatively few leave Afghanistan to recount these incidents to the press or others. Nonetheless, accounts of chemical attacks have been collected, notably by the U.S. government, which has noted the most

Mujahideen rebels wear gas masks stolen from Soviet troops to protect themselves from chemical and toxin weapons used against them by the occupying forces. © Ken Guest/ Keystone Features/Getty Images.

reliable of them (Department of State Report to the Congress, March 22, 1982, and Department of State Report, November 29, 1982). According to such accounts, the use of chemical weapons has continued from the summer of 1979 up through the date covered in the latest reports, October, 1982 [Even before the invasion of December 1979, large numbers of Soviet troops and officers were actively participating in the effort to crush the anti-Communist resistance in Afghanistan.]. In the spring of 1982 Undersecretary Walter Stoessel testified that through an analysis of accounts, a minimum of 3,042 deaths in Afghanistan could be attributed to the use of chemical weapons by the Soviet military. It should be remembered, of course, that in cases where no witnesses survived or made contact to describe an attack, no statistics could be compiled.

Corroborating Testimony from Doctors, Aid Workers, and Soviet Soldiers

The second category of evidence—the testimony of physicians and refugee workers—is easier to buttress: their statements of difficult and unusual symptoms—including readily observable skin lesions—are not only supported by photographic evidence, but are consistent with what is known about the physical effects of various chemical agents, including lethal agents, such as the nerve gases and the recently discovered trichothecene toxins. Medical examinations have also revealed neurological impairment, including paralysis in a number of cases; blistering; skin lesions; and hemorrhaging.

Statements of Soviet army defectors and Afghan army (Kabul regime) defectors, as well as captured Soviet personnel, have provided important additional evidence, along with descriptions of deployment, storage, decontaminating agents used, and confirmation of eyewitness reports of certain attacks. The accounts given by one particular Soviet soldier, Anatoly Sakharov, received an unusual amount of press attention several months ago [in 1982], particularly because of his statement that among a variety of chemical agents being used were picrine and picric acid—seen by some observers as explaining some of the more bizarre symptoms that frequently have been reported.

Physical and Photographic Evidence of Soviet Chemical Attacks

Obtaining, let alone analyzing, physical samples of the agents used has been extraordinarily difficult. Not surprisingly, those able to survive a chemical attack are not likely to use the occasion to collect samples—even if they are equipped and able to do so safely, which is seldom the case. Even when physical samples may be collected, bringing them out of Afghanistan is not an easy matter. Significantly, however, physical evidence in the form of residue of a chemical agent was found on the surface of a captured Soviet gas mask, and chemical analysis of that material showed the presence of trichothecene mycotoxins, leading the Department of State and other observers to conclude—piecing this together with other evidence—that those mycotoxins have been used in Afghanistan since at least 1980. (Use of those mycotoxins has also been traced to Soviet-client forces in Laos and Cambodia.)

Least available, not surprisingly, is photographic evidence of chemical weapons attacks, even though, for some of the most skeptical, only such evidence is deemed adequate. Despite the difficulties, film footage taken by the Dutch journalist Bernd de Bruin, who witnessed an attack, showed a Soviet MI-24 helicopter dropping canisters that produced a dirty yellow cloud, as well as the blackened, bloated, rapidly-decomposing body of a victim de Bruin knew to be alive less than twenty-four hours earlier.

The evidence clearly leads to the inescapable conclusion that chemical weapons are being used in Afghanistan by Soviet forces. And, it should be emphasized, it is not on any one single piece of evidence that this conclusion rests, but on the combined, cumulative evidence which confirms what might otherwise remain open to some question.

Chemical Weapons Mesh Well with Soviet Tactics and Goals

The use of chemical weapons is illegal, morally reprehensible, and risky. Why then, one naturally is led to ask, would the Soviets do it? Without the ability to listen in to Kremlin chitchat, we can do little other than speculate. But Soviet behavior does give us some insight, and the strong reactions the Soviets have shown to revelations of their use of chemical weapons make it clear they are sensitive about this—defensive in their denials, and unwilling to permit any sort of impartial investigation on territory they control. (The Soviet opposition to U.N. investigations, their rather lame and ludicrous rebuttal, in a report purportedly done by the Soviet Academy of Sciences last year, to the charges, and their refusal to permit the U.N. investigative team to enter Afghanistan are among the indications.)

It seems likely that, in the first place, the Soviets did not think it probable they would be caught out. In the second place, even if they were caught—that is, if reports of their use of chemical weapons did come out—they believed those reports would be unverifiable, leading to widespread skepticism as to whether such weapons were indeed actually being employed. Finally, they appear to believe that even if it should be widely accepted that they are using chemical/toxin weapons, no one would do much about it. (Unfortunately, this is indeed what has happened—at least, thus far.)

More practically, chemical weapons are militarily useful in the rough, mountainous and difficult terrain of Afghanistan, where the Afghan freedom fighters have the natural advantage of knowing their own land, and where they have the support of the vast majority of the population. In fighting such as guerrilla conflict chemical weapons can give a military advantage to the attackers. In addition, they can be used as a terror weapon, not only against the combatants but against the civilian population that is also resisting, if only passively, the occupation of their country.

T-2 Trichothecene Mycotoxin and Soviet "Yellow Rain"

In September 1981 US Secretary of State Alexander Haig revealed that Soviet-backed forces had deployed mycotoxin-based "yellow rain" biochemical weapons in Laos and Cambodia. Haig reiterated and expanded these allegations in a report submitted to Congress in March 1982, and his successor—Secretary of State George Shultz—continued to repeat and expand these charges, which became the basis of the widely reported assertion that the Soviet Union was researching and stockpiling such chemical and biological weapons.

During the Cold War, civilians and soldiers targeted by Soviet and Soviet-supported troops reported a variety of chemical attacks in which they were sprayed by a viscous yellow fluid, often falling in small droplets from a high altitude. Following contact with this yellow rain, victims reported a variety of symptoms, including seizures, blindness, bleeding from the nose and gums, and skin irritation. There were also purported fatalities resulting from contact with the yellow rain. Initial analysis of yellow rain samples, as well as bodily fluids and tissue from victims, revealed small traces of the mycotoxin T-2. This naturally occurring compound is produced by some species of the *Fusarium* fungus, which can infect whole grains. T-2 is known to be harmful to humans and animals, causing

The Soviets Used Afghanistan as a Testing Ground for New Weapons

Too, when chemical weapons are used persistently, they can deny access to areas—particularly when, as is the case in Afghanistan, the victims have no protective gear or equipment. Finally, the evidence that a wide variety of chemical agents is being used, including some that have not been seen before, and additional evidence that Soviet chemical weapons specialists have been collecting data following attacks, leads to the conclusion that the

a diverse array of symptoms. The Soviet Union suffered an outbreak of T-2 poisoning just after WWII when flour ground from *Fusarium*-tainted grain was inadvertently used to bake bread. In the aftermath, Soviet scientists were known to have considered the possible military applications of weaponized T-2 mycotoxin.

Independent scientific analysis ultimately found that the samples of the alleged yellow rain chemical agent recovered from Laos, Cambodia, and Afghanistan contained digested pollen from a variety of local plant species, and were almost certainly honeybee excrement. Several subsequent incidents of yellow rain—including one such event documented near Sangrampur, India, in 2002—have proven to be mass honeybee defecation events.

The near consensus in the scientific community today is that the yellow rain samples—purported to be evidence of a secret Soviet T-2 mycotoxin chemical weapon—were almost certainly honeybee feces. Although both eyewitness reports and forensic evidence supporting the existence of a Soviet mycotoxin chemical weapon were ultimately determined to be highly unreliable, the US government has never publicly withdrawn or formally dismissed these accusations, considering the incidents "unresolved." Nonetheless, credible reports gathered at the time indicate that the Soviet Union had stockpiled traditional chemical weapons, trained their forces to use and handle such agents, and equipped them to do so. The Soviet Union is known to have used "non-lethal" chemical agents in Afghanistan very similar to those deployed by US forces in Vietnam.

Soviets are not simply using chemical and toxin agents for military advantage, but are experimenting on a scale that would otherwise be impossible.

The reports of a wide variety of chemical weapons deployed in a number of different ways buttress this conclusion: that the Soviets are using Afghanistan as a testing ground for various weapons. In addition to incapacitants and lethal chemical weapons dispersed by aircraft, rockets, or projectiles there have been frequent reports of poisons used in the waterways (including the underground irrigation systems), poison bullets and flechettes, and poisons used to contaminate food supplies. That the Soviet leadership cares so little for human life may not come as a surprise to many who are aware of the history of the treatment of Soviet citizens, but such experimentation on the people of an independent country already brutalized by a Soviet-sponsored coup, followed by the invasion and occupation by Soviet forces, is nonetheless extraordinary and monstrous.

Implications of the Soviet Practice of Deploying Chemical Weapons

The Soviet use of chemical weapons in Afghanistan is a clear-cut violation of the 1925 Geneva Protocol, to which the Soviet Union is a signatory; their use of toxin weapons (the trichothecene toxins) is a violation of the 1972 Biological and Toxin Weapons Convention to which they are also a signatory. And, perhaps even more important than the violation of two international accords (important though they are) is the fact that the use of chemical weapons is also a violation of the customary international law prohibiting use of chemical weapons that has evolved over the years—and that the Soviet Union has acknowledged. The Soviets' disregard for agreements they have signed and for humanitarian international law may indeed not be surprising for those who have seen other aspects of Soviet behavior in Afghanistan; but it is nonetheless disquieting.

For those who hope to see progress made in the area of arms control, the egregious violations of already existing and important arms control agreements can only lead to a pessimistic outlook. For those with hopes of seeing an end to the Soviet occupation of Afghanistan, the revelations of the lengths to which Soviet policymakers are willing to go to keep their hold on Afghanistan—in the face of international opprobrium—can only be profoundly discouraging.

The Soviet use of chemical weapons in Afghanistan should be a matter of deep concern for all citizens—not just those with a strong interest in Afghanistan—because of the implications this use has for our relations with the Soviet Union and for the future of agreements with the Soviets. But at the same time, even as we look at these broader geopolitical considerations, we should not forget that there are victims, that there is an immense amount of suffering. The issue of the use of chemical weapons must be seen, first and foremost, as a humanitarian issue.

The Soviet Occupiers Derailed Afghanistan's Justice System

Michael Barry, Omar Babrakzai, and Ghafoor Yussofzai

The following viewpoint consists of testimony given before the New York Bar Association's Committee of International Human Rights on January 28, 1983. The witnesses detail the ways in which Soviet occupying forces derailed Afghanistan's existing, functional judicial system. They give examples of the system put in place by the Soviets, which featured arbitrary detentions and executions, convictions in the absence of any investigation, extensive use of torture, and the collective punishment of entire families or villages for the actions of a few individuals. Michael Barry is an Islamic scholar and specialist in Afghan affairs; Omar Babrakzai is a former judge of the Kabul High Court of Appeals; and Ghafoor Yussofzai served as a resistance commander in northeastern Afghanistan. Mr. Barry also served as the Afghan translator at the hearing.

*M*ichael Barry: The witnesses our commission selected are all here with us today. Mr. Omar Babrakzai, a graduate of the University of Paris and a former judge of the Kabul High Court of Appeals, has carried out extensive investigation of the use of antipersonnel mines against the civilian population in his native prov-

Dagens Nyheter (Today's News), "Atrocities and Violations of Human Rights and International Law in Afghanistan," *World Affairs Journal*, Winter 1982–1983. Copyright © 1983 by the World Affairs Institute. All rights reserved. Reproduced by permission.

ince of Pakhtya in southeastern Afghanistan. These include booby traps shaped to look like alarm clocks or pens or match boxes, and small, butterfly-shaped antipersonnel mines no larger than a human hand, which are scattered in rural areas where the flocks are ravaged, and small children who guard the flocks usually lose their feet or—if they fall hands first—lose their hands. These things are completely camouflaged: in desert territory, they are khaki-colored, while in foliage, pastureland, or forest they are green. In any case, they blend perfectly with the landscape. The judge has also located the only known case of a booby trap which did not self-destruct enough so that it could not be recognized; it was the shell of an alarm clock that had been rigged to explode in somebody's hands, and we have a photo of it. These were also placed in houses: Soviet troops often chased frightened villagers from their homes, and while they were gone, placed such booby traps in mattresses, where they were sure to inflict severe injuries against women and children.

Here is also Mr. Ghafoor Yussofzai. He is a resistance commander in northeastern Afghanistan, in Takhar Province, which borders the Soviet Union. He has terrible things to say about events which he has either witnessed directly or of which he has very close knowledge. Before the Soviet invasion, Mr. Yussofzai obtained a degree in law at Kabul University and was employed in a government ministry until he decided to join the resistance and take up arms against the occupying forces. . . .

How the Soviet Invasion Affected Afghan Courts

Omar Babrakzai: In the name of God, most merciful and compassionate.

It is a very great honor for me as your colleague, a man of your age. I studied law at the same time as you and to be able to sit with my colleagues today and to tell them our story of what our people are suffering is very deeply gratifying to me. I am grateful for this opportunity to state my case in your assembly along with my fellow resistance fighters who are here from the interior of Afghanistan. You are greatly to be honored, because your preoccupation is the defense of the rights of man. The profession of lawyer is one of defense of human rights. It is a high position.

I beg permission to describe the legal system of Afghanistan as it existed before the Russian invasion, and to contrast it with its present status today.

Before the Russians entered Afghanistan, the judiciary was very properly organized, and was completely independent of the legislative branch, which in turn was completely independent of the government. We had complete separation of powers. In Afghan courts two systems of law prevailed, the traditional Islamic law (*Shari 'yat*) for certain affairs and, separate from this, civil codes for certain civil affairs. Trials had a triple process, first the trial, then the appeal, and lastly the case was carried up to the third supreme judgment.

The Russian presence has ended this delicate system of checks and balances and abolished the independence of the judiciary. Russians were appointed to sit as advisors on the Supreme Court; Russian advisors watched over the proceedings of every court and gave their opinions. Actually, as a consequence of the entry of the Red Army into Afghanistan, it is not proper any longer to speak of such things as courts, lawyers, or judicial proceedings in our country.

Arbitrary Arrest, Torture, and Execution

I would like to give some examples of what are known as judicial proceedings in our country today. People who express dissent or hold views opposed to the present [Russian-installed] government—without having committed any crime whatsoever, and without ever appearing before a court—are hauled from their homes in the middle of the night. They are first sent to the torture chambers of the [Communist-created and Soviet-supervised] Kabul security police, which is known as Khad. After this they are sent to Pul-i-Charkhi "detention center," or concentration camp, ten kilometers east of Kabul. Every night between 200 and

Mujahideen prisoners walk inside the Pol-i-Charki prison in Kabul in April 1992. Prisoners from the Soviet occupation were released in large numbers after the mujahideen government took power in Afghanistan in 1992. © AP Images/Liu Heung Shing.

300 people are told that they are being released from detention, and are escorted to a former artillery field known as the Polygon, where they are executed.

These people have never seen a lawyer and have no recourse to the law. They are not brought before a court, nor told why they are arrested nor why they are being sent to execution. They are simply put to death. Families are not told whether those in prison have been executed or are still alive. They gather around the prison doors and ask for news of their loved ones, and are never told whether this or that relative has been executed or is still alive.

Barry: I add my own testimony to this, which is that 13,000 people were executed in Kabul between late 1978 and early 1979[1] and the list of the executed was only published all at once, posted in the various post offices so that the families would know that there was no point any longer in coming to the prison to bring packages, parcels of food and clothing and to find out what was going on. Listing the dead only occurred once; usually one does not know whether prisoners are dead or alive. I will add that Miss Farida Ahmadi has said that she has no knowledge about whether her family is alive or dead. Nor does Mr. Yussofzai know whether his brother, a student in economics at Kabul University, who was arrested two years ago, is alive or dead.

Forced Confessions and Secret Detention

The Soviets have brought into our country implements such as electric chairs, where the shock is such that it will project the prisoner straight out of the chair when he receives a bolt, or tables of torture through which electric current runs and subjects them to severe pain. People who do not confess under such torture—95 to 99 percent of them undergo such torture until they die. People who do confess must sign their name to a list of crimes to which they have confessed to be party. For this confession they are condemned to death and executed.

However, there is a third category concerning petty civil cases which, of course, do not go through this process. These consist of such things as contract disputes between merchants, and anything disconnected from military or political matters. They usually go through the normal process of law such as had existed before.

Babrakzai: I can give you the example of my own elder brother, who was arrested on the very day when pro-Soviet forces took power during the coup, on April 27, 1978. He was one of the first to be arrested. For four months I went from prison to prison in Kabul and the surrounding area asking about him, but could find out nothing. After four months, a strip of paper was smuggled to me, a little strip of paper on which was my brother's handwriting and signature asking for a parcel of clothing for Pul-i-Charkhi concentration camp. Since that day I have received no news of my brother, and do not know whether he is alive or dead.

Soviets Dictate Legal Decisions at Almost Every Level

I mentioned this first class of people, who are arrested without having committed any recognizable crime whatsoever. Of course, there is a second category of people who are accused of specific acts—or "crimes," if you like: people who, the government is convinced, are guilty in their eyes of some specific act, are carried to the underground cells of the Interior Ministry, which are occupied by the security police—Khad—where they must submit to torture. Of course, the confessions of these people are extorted under torturer[2]—electro-shocks, beatings, burning of the flesh with cigarettes or other things, application of electric prods, stripping of the skin—and worse.

Yet even in this category of petty cases, the views of a Soviet advisor are requested, and are binding in all cases. The views of the Soviet advisor will sway the case—for example, in a lawsuit involving somebody who is thought to be a merchant belonging to the so-called "capitalist class," even though the law may be on his side in a particular case, there is very little chance that he will ever be able to prove his case in court.

I would just like to submit to you by way of example a case that was brought before the court not long ago.

Barry: The judge is referring to the time when he was still on the court, even though this was after the pro-Soviet 1978 coup.

Babrakzai: A group of workers in the city were having lunch, and they must have suffered some kind of food poisoning. They were taken to the hospital and one of them died. The only person who was hauled before a court was one of the workers who had himself been sick and who, as they were told, had been guilty of having bought meat [for the lunch] in the bazaar. The Justice Minister ordered that this man be convicted and executed.

Convictions Without Investigations
Barry: In other words, he was accused of poisoning another person?

Babrakzai: This was the person who had cut up the meat, divided it and shared it with the group, so he was to be convicted.

I was the judge on this case, and I said, "I cannot accept such a judgment—when a person buys meat in a shop the day before, and just for this you are going to condemn him to death? I cannot accept this case." There had been no medical expertise, no autopsy performed to prove the person who died had actually been poisoned by a certain chemical. There was no proof whatsoever that this was a case of deliberate poisoning. In terms of law, the whole matter seemed to be extremely strange, considering that nothing was actually proved and that there was nothing but rumor. But the Soviet advisor said that the court must set an example that crimes are punished, the court has said that a man will die as a consequence of what has been described as a crime, and the important point here is the example to be set. So the man was condemned.

I went to the Ministry of Justice, and pleaded by saying that the man who was condemned to death belonged to the social class of workers. I explained that the society they were bringing about was to be a workers' society, and asked them why they were making an example out of a worker. "Why do you want to kill a working man? All I want from you is at the very least to carry out proper investigations and to prove satisfactorily that there has been a case of deliberate poisoning." I did manage to have an investigation carried out: an autopsy was performed, and the laboratory confirmed that it was not the meat but the potatoes that were eaten with the meat which were bad. Since this was something entirely natural, the man had really died of natural causes. Thanks to my intercession, it was possible to save the man's life and he was acquitted.

"You People Have No Right to Possess Such Things"

I have given this example, though it may be a ridiculous little case, just to show you how Soviet advisors weigh on particular cases throughout Afghanistan's courts today. I will not take up all your time by telling of the many hundreds of such cases that are submitted to Afghan courts every day.

Actually the examples of what is going on in Afghanistan today belong on another level, and this is what I really must tell you about. Fortunately, today 80 percent of Afghan soil is in the hands of the resistance movement. Thus, in 80 percent of Afghanistan's territory, justice is actually administered by the resistance movement itself according to traditional tribal law. Most of the cases now tried by country courts in resistance-held areas are of an entirely peaceful nature—litigation and wrangling between various plaintiffs—and these are settled peacefully. We in the Muslim Unity of Afghan Mujahidin[3] have in our unified political structure an Office of the Supreme Court, and we apply the law that was formerly the supreme law of the Afghan state. . . .

But as regards protection afforded by law in any area which is controlled by Soviet troops, I can assure you that there is no such thing any longer as the rule of law and order. In any area, especially urban areas, controlled by the Soviet army, government, Party, or Soviet military personnel have the complete right to arrest anybody they choose, search them, throw them into jail, and kill them.

Private homes are not protected by law: they can be violated, visited, searched at will. The reason given for house searches is a search for weapons. However, when houses are searched and valuables are found—whether money, jewelry or what have you—they are confiscated. The reason given is that "you people have no right to possess such things."

Soviet Cultural and Religious Persecution

I would now like to leave the floor to my associates, who can tell you of actual Soviet atrocities, violations of human rights, and violations of the legal code, whether of war or peace. These people can tell you in their own voices what they have actually witnessed. . . .

Mr. Ghafoor Yussofzai: In the name of God, most merciful and most compassionate, to Him we turn, and to our Prophet.

With your permission, Mr. Chairman, and all of you in the legal profession—the Soviets have violated every kind of international law by invading our country in this way. The Soviets are signatories to the Charter of the United Nations, and this they have violated. Every sort of treaty existing between the Soviet Union and Afghanistan to which the Russians affixed their signature has been violated by the Soviets themselves in the occupation of our country. And worse than this, every kind of elementary human right has been trampled on by the occupation forces.

They deny us the freedom to worship and to profess our faith: they belittle and humiliate our religious beliefs. Despite the fact that this war is taking place between a world power and a tiny underdeveloped nation—even with the balance of power so firmly on their side—nevertheless, they violate every rule of war.

Soviet Use of Collective Punishment

I would like to give you a number of examples. Today, 80 percent of Afghan soil is in the hands of resistance forces. We administer justice and law in those territories which we control. Such cases which are submitted to us, whether civil or military, are pleaded before duly appointed judges. Nobody is convicted, condemned, or sentenced to death without having been tried and proved guilty before responsible appointed judges. In those cases in which we feel that we do not have sufficient information, or in which an appeal was made, then, as His Honor Judge Babrakzai said, we from our local district courts send the person on to be tried by the higher court which is at the political center. The basic legal code today in that part of Afghanistan which is held by resistance forces is based on the Koran and on the traditional religious law of Islam.

The Soviets are practicing collective guilt. In other words, suppose I've committed a crime myself, personally; if they can't find me, then other people are punished for the crime. For example—I myself don't consider this a crime, of course—I have taken up arms to defend the independence of my country. My brother did not do so. But it is my brother, a student at the university, who was arrested several years ago and who has disappeared from sight. My wife and two children were executed by firing squad.

Execution of Children and Elderly

[At this point, Mr. Yussofzai began reading a list of specific atrocities:] On January 15, 1980, [three weeks after the Soviet invasion] just above the provincial district capital of Kunduz in northeastern Afghanistan, in the subprefecture of Hazrat-i-Imam-Sahib [close to the Soviet border, on the main invasion route.—Ed.] in the village of Chukhurkhalbad, 480 people, including women, children, and the elderly, were crushed by Soviet tanks, and those who survived were executed by firing squad. Those, however, who were bearing arms, and who were captured by Soviet forces, were tied to the tanks and dragged behind them until they died. . . .

On December 1, 1981, in two villages in the area of the district capital of Taluqan in northeastern Afghanistan, five elderly were seized. They were asked, "Where are the bandits?" (That's what the Russians call resistance fighters.) They said "We don't know." They were killed by a bullet which caused their bodies to decompose as if they had been burned.

We found their bodies only four hours after execution, and they were decomposing as if they had been burned. However, we have been able to recover some of these cartridges from their bodies and have submitted them for analysis to the Permanent People's Court which was held in Paris last December; they are currently in the laboratory.

On January 3, 1982, in the subdistrict capital of Khwaja-i-Ghar in the prefecture of Dasht-i-argh, villagers were bombed and I have direct knowledge of the death of 250 people. In another village, 26 people, without judgment of any kind, were lined up and executed. Ninety people at that time were cast into the river which forms the boundary between Afghanistan and the Soviet Union. [This is the Amu Darya or Oxus River.] The Soviet soldiers took pot shots at anybody's head which popped out of the water, as if they were duck shooting. . . .

In the main square of the city of Khanabad on [January 6, 1982] was a bus containing twenty people, which was about to leave. The Soviets surrounded the bus and prevented anybody from getting off. They set it on fire and burned alive the twenty passengers, who included four children and two women. After bombing the city, the Soviets occupied it.

In March 1982 in the village of Sabsposh-i-Kalatan, two children, Sultan and Wazalmai—seven and eight years old, the sons of His Holiness Abdul Qader, a cleric—were seized. They were condemned because their father happened to be a resistance fighter. They were told, "You have given food to resistance fighters."

These children had toy rifles made of wood. The Afghan government translator who was with the Russian forces asked the children what they used toy guns for. "We use these guns to fight against the Russians," said the children. Russian troops doused the children with gasoline and set them on fire.

I submitted this particular case to the Inquiry Commission of the Permanent People's Tribunal which came to Peshawar, Pakistan. One hundred witnesses testified to the veracity of this event, and you have here Mr. Michael Barry, who was a member of the Inquiry Commission, and who can testify that he was able to interrogate with some rigor the 100 witnesses to this particular event of the burning alive of the two children.

The crimes that I have just mentioned occurred only in one corner of the country where my resistance forces can be directly aware of such things. I am only telling you about what I know directly, having witnessed it myself, or from what I have been told by the people working with me.

What more can I tell you about Soviet war crimes? You know what it's all about. You know, the Communists promised that they would give us bread, housing, and clothing: they promised us lodging and they gave us graves. They promised us clothing and they gave us winding sheets; and in place of bread, they gave us poison gas.

The Afghan People Only Seek Justice

Barry: Mr. Yussofzai has not only suffered bullet wounds, but he was involved in a chemical attack which has left these marks on his body. [Mr. Yussofzai removed his shirt to show the inflamed patches on his skin as well as a Soviet bullet still lodged in one arm.]

Yussofzai: The Soviet Union is saying, "We have come into Afghanistan to protect the Afghans from the attacks of Chinese, Pakistanis, and American soldiers. We are only in Afghanistan—100,000 Soviet troops—to defend the people of Afghanistan from these foreigners." I can assure you that *no foreign troops whatsoever*—no foreign country whatsoever—has given the Afghan people any kind of help at all, except the Islamic government of Pakistan, which has given to our refugees asylum and sanctuary, and has extended to them humanitarian assistance.

These weapons which we have, we have seized from the Russians with our own empty hands, and by suffering wounds and great pain. I still have Russian lead in my body, and until I have driven Russian forces out of my homeland, I will not pull it out of my body. My skin now bears the traces of a chemical warfare attack. But how long are we going to have to come before you and weep? How long are we going to have to tell you what our country is suffering?

I have come as an Afghan resistance fighter, but I am also a student of law, and of your proud nation and of the government of America. I lay this case before you:

Do not leave our oppressed nation alone and defenseless before a group of criminals. Help us with weapons. Help us so that we shall not starve to death. I assure you most solemnly that as long as there is a single individual left alive in Afghanistan, that one individual will do everything he can to prevent Afghanistan from being occupied by the Soviets.

Notes

1. I.e., between the Communist coup of April 27, 1978, and the entry of the Soviet forces, which installed [Babrak] Karmal. In the August 1982 issue of *Commentary*, Barry noted that Karmal accused his predecessors, [Noor Mohammad] Taraki and [Hafizullah] Amin, of killing *one million* people. The 13,000 mentioned here are only those whose names were posted in October 1979; their ages ranged from 12 up.
2. Torture was outlawed in Afghanistan in 1905. The 1964 constitution specified civil rights modeled on the U.S. Bill of Rights.
3. A coalition of many of the major resistance groups inside Afghanistan with the three moderate groups based in Pakistan.

VIEWPOINT 5

Afghanistan Needed Humanitarian Aid as Well as Military Support to Halt Genocide

Edward Girardet

Journalist Edward Girardet has reported from war-torn regions throughout Africa and Asia since the 1970s. He is the author of Killing the Cranes: A Reporter's Journey Through Three Decades of War in Afghanistan. *In the following viewpoint, first published in 1985, Girardet offers in-depth analysis of the "total warfare" waged against the Afghan people by the Soviet Union. This strategy was called "migratory genocide," which meant not only indiscriminately killing civilians, but purposefully displacing the entire noncombatant population, shifting them into Soviet controlled zones, and dismantling their indigenous culture. Girardet asserts that because the Soviet goal was to completely disrupt life in Afghanistan, simply supplying military aid was insufficient; Afghanistan badly needed a concerted, internationally-supported reconstruction effort, which was not forthcoming.*

The Soviet Antonov reconnaissance plane droned into view shortly after dawn. It swept past Mir Samir, a towering, snowcapped peak on the southern fringe of the Hindu Kush mountains, and traversed the 14,000-foot-high Chamar Pass.

The Antonov was no doubt tracking a stream of refugees, many of them farmers and nomads who were fleeing to Pakistan, still several weeks' trek away, with their camels, horses, sheep, and goats. They were attempting to escape the increasing pressures of war: repeated Red Army ground and air assaults, conscription drives by the Afghan security forces, and famine caused by the destruction of food sources.

Total Warfare Was Poorly Reported in U.S. Media

It was mid-August last year [1984], and I was accompanying a two-man British CBS-TV team on my sixth trip through Afghanistan since the Soviet invasion on December 27, 1979. We were on our way to the fertile Panjshair Valley, a prominent resistance stronghold, where the Afghan guerrillas, the mujahideen, were trying to stave off the Soviet Union's seventh offensive against the region, a massive operation involving a combined Soviet-Afghan force of more than 20,000 men. A week later I passed through the Chamar area again, on my way back to Pakistan. Dozens of mutilated animal carcasses, twisted metal pots, scorched clothing, torn saddles, and a boy's tattered slingshot littered the ground. The dead had been buried in a yawning bomb crater, their bodies covered with a tarpaulin, upon which stones were piled, in the Muslim manner. The attack was recorded with a single prayer flag—a piece of green, pink, and orange cloth hanging from a wooden tent pole. The survivors straggled into Pakistan in late September.

The Chamar Pass massacre shows just what kind of war the Kremlin is waging in Afghanistan. By slaughtering innocent human beings, bombing farms, despoiling crops, killing animals, and wrecking fragile irrigation systems, the USSR seeks not only to punish the local population for its resistance sympathies, but also to totally disrupt the economic and social infrastructure of the guerrilla-held areas, which represent well over 80 percent of the country. The Kremlin has made it clear that it is fully prepared to pursue this goal for years, if not decades.

Although the Soviet occupation of Afghanistan is one of the most extensive strategic wars today, American press coverage—particularly television—has been poor. The European media have been considerably more resourceful. The physical remoteness, rugged terrain, and cultural complexity of Afghanistan account for some of the neglect. Situations change rapidly in a matter of days or hours from valley to valley, and it can take weeks to send out hand-carried dispatches or film reports from the interior. Still, the neglect is probably due as much to a lack of editorial resolve as it is to the dangers and difficulties of covering the war. At present, no American newspaper, magazine, or wire service has a full-time correspondent reporting on Afghanistan. Yet the war continues to escalate. The Soviets have become mired in a counterinsurgency campaign that has already lasted longer than World War II; and their continuing presence in Afghanistan poses a grave threat to the regional stability of South Asia and the Gulf, and ultimately to Western interests.

The Soviet Military Tactic of "Migratory Genocide"

At present, the Soviet Union maintains an expeditionary force of more than 115,000 troops (increased from 85,000 in the early days of the occupation), which controls the cities, air bases, main highways, and certain strategic points. The Soviets have experienced continuing setbacks with their armed forces. The desertion-ridden Afghan army, once over 100,000 strong, can barely muster 35,000 men at any one time, and the Soviets have been forced to rely on highly paid militiamen to bolster local security. The Red Army, too, has been replacing its largely conscript army—which, Soviet deserters claim, is suffering from low morale and a high rate of drug abuse—by more motivated professionals. Still, the Soviets have a number of obvious advantages over the poorly equipped, disorganized guerrillas. They can draw from a lethal arsenal of weapons ranging from the rapid-fire Mi-24 helicopter gunship to the highly maneuverable SU-25

Soviet soldiers surveil the highlands of Afghanistan while fighting Islamic rebels. Soviet troops used a variety of military strategies against Afghans. © AP Images/Estate of Alexander Sekretarev.

fighter-bomber—not to mention a Machiavellian array of subversive tactics by the KGB [the Soviet security agency].

What's more, the Red Army's ability to conduct a large-scale counterinsurgency war has steadily improved. Deploying well-trained commandos and tactics suited to mountain guerrilla warfare in the northeastern areas of Afghanistan, or armor and air-supported Talashi (cordon-and-thump attacks) in the more exposed desert zones, the Soviets have sought to destroy the most defiant of the resistance's vast patchwork of 300-odd guerrilla fronts. Nevertheless, the war has remained a grueling military standoff. The Soviets may be fighting better in certain areas, but so are the guerrillas.

It is on the civilian front that the Afghans are in danger of losing the war. The Soviet leadership has realized that it is in every sense a "people's war," and has adopted an unrestrained policy of what has become known as "migratory genocide"—the killing or forcing out of people suspected of supporting the mujahideen. "It does not take much to realize what the Russians are trying to do," said a member of the Swedish Committee for Afghanistan in Peshawar, Pakistan. "They are turning every region that does not bend to their will into a wasteland."

Some five million people, one-quarter to one-third of the pre-war population, have fled to Pakistan, Iran, and elsewhere. Countless others have sought refuge in the mountains or in Kabul and a few other overcrowded Soviet-controlled cities. Although reliable figures are virtually impossible to come by, hundreds of thousands of men, women, and children are believed to have been killed or to have died as a direct consequence of the war.

The Soviet Union's commitment to Afghanistan continues to rise—not only in the number of lives lost, anywhere from 10,000 to 20,000 Soviet troops since the invasion, but also in the economic resources used to prop up the Babrak Karmal regime in Kabul. For the sake of appearances, the Kremlin still seeks to uphold the myth that its "limited military contingent" is there to assist "independent" Afghanistan against what it describes as "subversive bandit forces" of outside "reactionary" or "imperialist" powers. But it has become increasingly apparent that Moscow's occupation is intended to bring about the eventual annexation of Afghanistan—either partial, leaving a rump state to satisfy Third World concerns about self-determination, or total annexation, another Soviet Socialist Republic.

The "Sovietization" of Afghanistan

The Soviets' domination of the Kabul government is almost complete. Soviet advisers now effectively control the decision-making in the ministries and the army, and they are in the process of "Sovietizing" virtually every aspect of society in the communist-occupied areas. . . . By offering financial incentives and privileges to tribal, religious, and guerrilla leaders, the Soviets hope to obtain active assistance—or at least neutrality—in defending the revolution. Indeed, they have established an elaborate network of informers that severely hampers the resistance. Earlier this year, one of Afghanistan's leading northern commanders,

Zabiullah, was reportedly killed after being betrayed by several of his comrades-in-arms, possibly at the instigation of the KHAD, the Afghan version of the KGB.

The Soviet strategy to broaden the Afghan Communist Party's base has been hindered somewhat by internecine strife between its two factions, the ruling pro-Soviet Parcham (Banner) and the more nationalist Khalq (Masses). By taking a long-term approach toward consolidating power, however, the Kremlin has recognized the need to cultivate whatever pools of support are available while laying the foundations for a "new" Afghanistan. As many as 50,000 teenagers have been sent to the USSR for training and indoctrination. Even if it takes a generation or two, the ultimate hope is to replace the present administration with appropriately groomed pro-Moscow cadres.

The first waves of "new" Afghans have already returned. It is not yet certain that Soviet methods of indoctrination will work. In the past, Afghans who studied in the USSR have returned home as ardent anti-Soviet nationalists because of the racial discrimination they experienced. And former Communists who have defected since the invasion have referred to the disparaging manner with which Soviet advisers treat their Afghan comrades.

The Afghans Seek Independence, Not a U.S. Ally

The stark realities of Moscow's determination to entrench have accentuated the loss of Afghanistan as a traditional buffer state between Russia and the Indian subcontinent. It has also resulted in Afghanistan's becoming an increasingly important part of U.S. foreign policy. If the latest reported figures are correct, the escalation of Central Intelligence Agency backing of the mujahideen ($325 million during the first five years, with $250 million earmarked for fiscal year 1985) now represents the largest U.S. covert operation since the Vietnam War. Congress, if no one else, is sure to demand more careful scrutiny of the issue.

The disputes currently center on the use of military aid to accomplish foreign policy objectives. Some would like to see the

CIA program used as a means of hitting the Russians with their own Vietnam. Representative Charles Wilson, who has pushed this approach, has been instrumental in lobbying for more effective weapons for the mujahideen such as advanced anti-aircraft guns. Some critics of the program have referred to the dangers of overtechnologizing "primitive people." Still others maintain that it is pointless to support a resistance that has no hope of winning against the Russians.

None of these arguments, though, take into account the objectives of the Afghans themselves. Mujahideen make it clear that they have no desire to be manipulated as an instrument of American retribution. And funneling weapons is not going to purchase pro-Americanism. Traditionally, Afghans have sought to maintain their independence by forging temporary alliances only if they are to their advantage. The present struggle is not aimed at "defeating" the Russians, but at making life so uncomfortable that they will leave, or at least negotiate. Many Afghans realize, too, that even if the Soviets withdraw, their country will have to live in the shadow of Russia. Neutrality toward the superpowers could prove to be their best course once again.

Furthermore, though living in a lesser developed country, Afghans reflect an amalgam of ancient civilizations and historical influences. The ethnic diversity of Afghanistan is comparable to that of Yugoslavia. The varied, often contentious Muslim population ranges from Sunni Pushtuns mainly to the east, to Tadjiks, Uzbeks, and Turkmen in the north, and Shiite Hazaras in the central highlands. "The West should try to understand that all we are trying to do is fight for our freedom," said Mohammed Es-Haq, foreign affairs representative for mujahideen leader Massoud. "We badly need help, but we also ask that one respect our rights as a people."

Though some Afghan groups could be aptly described as Islamic purists or radicals, it should not be assumed, as have some observers, that the Afghans' resistance is a collection of feuding tribesmen intent on preserving their old ways and

The Diversity of Afghanistan

Afghanistan has long been renowned for its ethnic and linguistic diversity. In fact, Westerners often attribute the region's notorious political instability to this diversity—an observation first set down in 1808 by Mountstuart Elphinstone, the first European diplomat to open relations with Afghanistan.

None of Afghanistan's ethnic groups—of which there are up-wards of a dozen—constitutes a majority. The largest, the Pash-tuns, have only rarely been estimated to include more than 45 per-cent of the nation's population, closely followed by the Tajiks (which are roughly 30 percent of the population), and Hazara (at 10 per-cent). Smaller distinct ethnic groups include Uzbeks, Aimaqs, Turk-men, Balochs, Ormurs, Gurjars, Brahui, Pashayi, Pamiri, Nuristani, and immigrant Arabs.

The Pashtuns are by far the most influential group and have been called "Afghans" since at least A.D. 300 (the nation of Afghani-stan takes its name from this tribe). They are Sunni Muslims, speak Pashtun, and are united by *Pashtunwali*, an unwritten ethical code mandating hospitality, justice, bravery, loyalty, righteousness, faith, courage, protection of women's honor, and protection of the weak. The mujahideen, Taliban, and current Afghan government have all

on bringing about another Khomeini-style revolution [The Ayatollah Khomehni was instrumental in the Iranian revolu-tion and served as the political and religious "Supreme Leader" of Iran from 1979 to 1989.] A largely peasant people, Afghans certainly remain highly conservative and devout in their jihad against the infidels from the north. But the consequences of war have ensured that things will never be the same again.

A recently formed centrist alliance of four resistance "funda-mentalist" and "moderate" parties now probably commands the bulk of Afghan popular support, leaving the two most extreme Islamic groups dangling. The graybeards, the traditional village leaders, have seen the fight against a modern, highly technologi-

been dominated by Pashtuns. The next largest ethnic groups are the Tajiks (who do not share a common ethnic identity but predominate in Afghanistan's largest cities and are 85 percent Sunni and 15 percent Shia) and the Hazara (a Shia minority concentrated in central Afghanistan).

While the Sunni/Shia division in Islam is inconsequential throughout much of the Muslim world—often equated to the division between Protestant and Catholic Christians—it has been a major source of strife in Iraq, Pakistan, and Afghanistan. It is estimated that roughly 90 percent of the Islamic world are Sunni Muslims.

Dari and Pashto are the official languages of Afghanistan. Dari is a dialect of Persian (spoken in Iran) and favored by Tajiks, Hazaras, Aimaks, and Kizilbash. Pashto (which shares a linguistic root with Persian, and thus with Dari) is the native language of the Pashtun ethnic group. The vast majority of Afghans are fluent in at least one of these two languages. Many also speak or read Arabic, the common language of the Muslim world.

Up to thirty minority languages are spoken in Afghanistan, including many language sub-families with small speaking populations only found in Afghanistan (such as the Nuristani languages of Ashkunu, Kamkataviri, Vasi-vari, Tregami, and Kalasha-ala). Many Afghans are also fluent in the languages commonly spoken in India and Pakistan: Urdu, Punjabi, Hindi, and English.

cal enemy evolve as a young man's war, resulting in an unprecedented handover of power. Thus, in a sense, Afghans in the guerrilla-controlled areas are witnessing a social revolution from below rather than one imposed from above, as the Communists are attempting in the cities. "Whereas the resistance used to represent backwardness and the Soviets' progress," says Olivier Roy, a French Foreign Ministry consultant on Afghan affairs, "now it is the guerrillas who stand for change and the Soviets for economic colonialism." As for the three million or so Afghans who have fled to Pakistan, they have been exposed for the first time to numerous outside influences: government administration, medical care, and, increasingly, education. And women have begun to assume new responsibilities in the absence of husbands and sons who are fighting, working, or dead.

Afghanistan Needs Humanitarian Aid, Not Just Military Support

As a resistance, the Afghans lack the political discipline or defined social concepts of other liberation movements. The mujahideen have far to go before they can hope to emulate the efficiency of the Viet Cong, the Eritrean People's Liberation Front, or Unita in Angola. Militarily, they appear to have sufficient good-quality small arms as well as a respectable array of heavy machine guns, light anti-aircraft weapons, and short-range mortars. But over the past few years, as the Soviets have upgraded their counter-insurgent tactics and materiel, the guerrillas have seen their defense capabilities whittled away. Hence the argument for better and more sophisticated arms.

In the past, most of the mujahideens' military aid has come from the Middle East, China, and the international arms market, a large portion of which is believed to have been purchased through American funding. Other arms, such as the Soviet-designed AK-47 or the more modern AK-74 assault rifles, have been obtained through capture or defection. But much of the weaponry intended for the interior never finds its way into guerrilla hands, largely because of poor distribution or outright corruption among Pakistani intermediaries and certain Afghans-in-exile. What material does arrive is reported to be of poor condition. . . . As a "front-line" state, the military regime of President Zia ul-Haq [of Pakistan] seeks, but has yet to receive, American guarantees of protection in the event of Soviet attack.

Still, it is crucial to note that the mujahideen suffer from a lamentable lack of training, organization, and qualified personnel. Simply providing money and weapons is not going to solve these problems. Military assistance should emphasize quality rather than quantity, with weapons best suited to the terrain and Afghan capabilities. Aid as well as training should be channeled not only through the political groups in Peshawar, but also directly to proven guerrilla commanders inside.

Most of the present controversy in Washington concerning CIA covert assistance overlooks the Afghans' humanitarian needs. Although international relief for Afghan refugees in Pakistan has been more than generous, little has gone to the six million to eight million inhabitants still struggling to survive inside the resistance-held areas of Afghanistan. The effect of denying relief to the Afghan interior is to erode local resistance by encouraging people to flee. For the moment, the mujahideen lack both the ability and the resources to assist civilians whose farms, crops, and livestock have been destroyed. Unlike the Soviets, who are also attempting to turn around the population with economic incentives and social reform, they have nothing to offer but war. The more perceptive commanders acknowledge that the present struggle may last "40 years," and that a sense of battle fatigue has already set in among many Afghans.

Some Afghan aid groups are now trying to help the guerrillas establish primary schools, agricultural centers, literacy classes, and health clinics inside Afghanistan. They have also suggested the creation of a Free Afghan University-in-exile for the several thousand former lecturers and students now milling about in Pakistan. Not only could this serve as a valuable resistance forum, but it could bolster guerrilla ranks with the qualified people it so desperately needs—notably doctors, teachers, and technicians.

The Soviet War's Effect on Journalism and Reporting

There is another way that the West can show its support for the Afghan resistance: by increasing the depth and extent of its press coverage of the war. As the effects of "migratory genocide" become more evident, the Kremlin would like nothing better than to contain all "unofficial" access to the country. The Soviets have exerted considerable pressure on the Pakistani government for allowing foreigners, whether journalists or relief workers, to cross the border. Last year the Soviets launched repeated air raids against the villages and refugee camps in Pakistan, killing more than 100 people. From the Soviet point of view, continued cross-border movements of outside observers are at least as threatening as the traffic of weapons. The Soviet ambassador in Islamabad [the capital of Pakistan] remarked in September 1984 that any reporters caught with the guerrillas would be "eliminated." When asked whether this constituted Kremlin policy, a Soviet embassy official in Washington responded that anyone "violating the territorial integrity of Afghanistan would have to face the consequences."

Denying or simply ignoring allegations of atrocities, the Kremlin continues to ignore demands by internationally recognized fact-finding commissions to enter Afghanistan. Only twice has the International Committee of the Red Cross been able to visit the Afghan capital, the last time in the fall of 1982, and then only under severe restrictions. "Ideally," said one European diplomat, "they would like to get on with their war without the outside world knowing." The difficulties in covering this kind of war are formidable, but the consequences of failing to do so are devastating.

The Soviet War in Afghanistan Was a Key Factor in the Collapse of the Soviet Union

Rafael Reuveny and Aseem Prakash

Rafael Reuveny is a professor at Indiana University's School of Public and Environmental Affairs. Aseem Prakash is a professor of political science at Washington University, focusing on international political economy, environmental issues, and the politics of non-governmental organizations. In the following viewpoint, the authors argue that the Soviet attempt to control Afghanistan through military occupation undermined the authority of the Soviet military among Communist Party leaders, military officers, enlisted soldiers, and civilians. Reuveny and Prakash maintain that the occupation drew into question the legitimacy of the Soviet Union, and this cultural destabilization accelerated a popular movement toward government openness and transparency (called glasnost in Russian). The authors assert that, although a small conflict in many regards, the botched occupation of Afghanistan was ultimately far more damaging to the Soviet Union than all other Cold War hostilities combined and was responsible for the final dissolution of the USSR in 1991.

Rafael Reuveny and Aseem Prakash, "The Afghanistan War and the Breakdown of the Soviet Union," *Review of International Studies*, no. 25, 1999. Copyright © 1999 British International Studies Association. Reprinted with the permission of Cambridge University Press.

Next to the two world wars, the rise and the breakdown of the Soviet Union are probably the most important political events of this century. This breakdown is often attributed to systemic and/or leadership factors. The Afghanistan war, as a key factor for the breakdown, is not emphasized. Systemic explanations suggest that collapse was inevitable due to domestic problems (such as inefficient central planning and ethnic problems) and/or structural problems (such as the Cold War and the increasing economic gap between the Soviet Union and the West). Leadership-based explanations emphasize the roles of political leaders (particularly [Mikhail] Gorbachev and [Soviet minister of foreign affairs Eduard] Shevardnadze) and the Soviet elites.

Yet systemic and leadership-based explanations inadequately address two key sets of questions. First, why did the physical break-up begin towards the end of the 1980s and the Soviet Union finally collapse in 1991? Why only in the mid-1980s did the Soviet leaders acknowledge the impossibility of sustaining their economic and foreign policies? Though the Soviet economy had deteriorated in the 1980s, it was not on the verge of an immediate breakdown. Moreover, in the 1970s and 1980s, the Soviets were, for the first time, on military parity with the United States.

Second, why did the Soviet leaders tolerate the non-Russian secessionist movements? Why did they not employ the Soviet Army to suppress these movements as they had done in Czechoslovakia (1968), Hungary (1956), and East Germany (1953)?

[Charles] Tilly attributes the breakdown of empires to major external or internal wars. He observes that between 1986 and 1992, the Soviet Union went through:

> [O]ne of Europe's more peculiar revolutions: the shattering of an empire and the dismantling of its central structure *without the direct impact of a war* . . . the costly stalemate in Afghanistan, itself a product of a hugely expensive Cold War

with the United States, provided the *closest equivalent* to those earlier empire-ending wars. [italics ours].

Yet, Tilly does not explain the etiology [cause] of the breakdown. We begin where Tilly left off.

Most scholars typically have viewed the Afghanistan war as a minor and containable conflict that had minimal impact on the basic institutions of the Soviet system. However, we view this war as one of the key causes, along with systemic and leadership-based factors, in the disintegration of the Soviet Union. The repeated failures in this war changed the Soviet leadership's perception of the efficacy of using force to keep non-Soviet nationalities within the Union (*perception effects*), devastated the morale and legitimacy of the army (*military effects*), disrupted domestic cohesion (*legitimacy effects*), and accelerated glasnost (*glasnost effects*). These effects operated synergistically. War failures weakened the military and conservative anti-reform forces and accelerated *glasnost* [increasingly open and transparent governance] and *perestroika* [economic and political reform]. Importantly, these failures demonstrated that the Soviet army was not invincible, thereby encouraging non-Russian republics to push for independence with little fear of a military backlash. . . .

Soviet Failure in Afghanistan Fundamentally Undermined the USSR

Major wars critically impact domestic politics by producing durable social changes and by redistributing political power among groups. An established literature explains how major wars may make as well as break states. Surprisingly, the extant explanations on the Soviet breakdown underemphasize the impact of the Afghanistan war.

The Soviets intervened in Afghanistan in December 1979. In retrospect, it was unthinkable in 1979 that the Soviet empire could collapse, let alone fall apart almost within a decade. Though the Afghanistan war initially was visualized by Soviet leaders as a small-scale intervention, it grew into a decade-long war involving nearly one million Soviet soldiers, killing and injuring some tens of thousands of them. During the early 1980s, the official Soviet media maintained that the Afghanistan Government had requested Soviet military assistance for humanitarian and non-combat tasks. Notwithstanding the media censorship, as the conflict escalated, and well before Gorbachev became the General Secretary of the Communist Party of the Soviet Union (CPSU), stories about combat casualties and the problems of disabled soldiers began appearing in spite of censorship.

Gorbachev, as the Secretary for Ideological Affairs under General Secretary [Konstantin] Chernenko, probably was not a participant in the decision processes leading to this intervention. He became General Secretary of the CPSU in 1985, roughly halfway through the Afghanistan war. We identify two phases in Gorbachev's policies towards the Afghanistan war and systemic reforms. In the first phase (summer 1984 to summer 1986), Gorbachev appeared to follow the policies of his predecessors on Afghanistan. To turn the tide of the war militarily, he named General Mikhail Zaitsev, one of the most illustrious Generals, to oversee the Soviet war efforts. At the domestic level, while Gorbachev mentioned the need for reforms, he did not champion them.

We view 1986 as the turning point in the Afghanistan war and, accordingly, as marking the second phase of Gorbachev's reform agenda. In 1986, the Mujaheddin (Afghan freedom fighters), now well armed with US-supplied surface-to-air missiles, rockets, mortars, and communication equipment, won many confrontations with the Soviet army. As successful ambushes of Soviet convoys became a daily phenomenon, the number of Soviet casualties mounted, the number of disabled soldiers seen in Soviet cities grew substantially, and the war veterans (*Afgantsy*) increasingly became part of the Soviet urban landscape. Since many *Afgantsy* belonged to the non-Russian nationalities, opposition to the war from citizens in non-Russian Soviet republics increased. Since their presence often was not acknowledged by the authorities, who wished to play down Soviet involvement in Afghanistan, these *Afgantsy* became bitter and openly critical of the Soviet leaders.

By late 1986, the Afghanistan war had significantly impacted on Soviet domestic politics. Anti-militarism became strong in the non-Russian Soviet republics. For non-Russians, the war became a unifying symbol of their opposition to Moscow's rule. The decision to withdraw from Afghanistan signalled Soviet military weakness and demonstrated that the army was vulnerable. By 1988, the war had changed the perceptions of Soviet leaders regarding the efficacy of using military force to hold the disintegrating country together.

This war also discredited the Soviet army. Since the Soviet army was the glue that held the diverse Soviet Republics together, its defeat in Afghanistan had profound implications for the survivability of the Soviet Union. Corruption, looting, and plundering by Soviet soldiers destroyed the army's moral legitimacy. The ethnic split in the army was accentuated when non-Russian soldiers, particularly those from Asian regions, displayed ambivalence toward fighting Afghans, deserted, and even revolted. Drug abuse was rising and, worse still, soldiers sold equipment to the Mujaheddin to obtain drugs, food, and electronic goods.

We categorize the war's effects into four types: (1) Perception effects; (2) Military effects; (3) Legitimacy effects; and (4) *Glasnost* effects. These categories are not equally important in explaining the impact of the Afghanistan war on Soviet politics and hence on Soviet breakdown. We consider the Perception and Military effects as being most important followed by Legitimacy effects, and finally *Glasnost* effects.

The Perception and Military effects refer to the discrediting of the Soviet army, perhaps the most important institution for holding the diverse country together, and to the changed Soviet leadership's perception on the efficacy of employing the army to quell secessionist movements in non-Russian republics. In particular, the *Afgantsy* played a key role in discrediting the army. Legitimacy effects describe the weakening of the army's and the country's internal cohesion. Finally, *Glasnost* effects refer to the impact of the war on accelerating *glasnost* by emboldening the media to report non-official war stories, thereby widening cleavages among various organs of the Soviet state.

Discrediting the Soviet Army

Soviet leaders before Gorbachev believed that they could, and should, employ the military to hold together their diverse country. In early 1983, while defending the Soviet Union's military involvement in Afghanistan, [Yury] Andropov, CPSU's General Secretary, observed that: "it took almost the entire Red Army fifteen years to subdue the rebellious khanates in the Soviet republics of Uzbekistan, Tajikistan and Kirgizstan". The Afghanistan war changed the Soviet leadership's perception of the efficacy of holding their diverse country together by using military force.

From 1979 to 1986, the war was portrayed by the Soviet media and leadership as an "international duty", and exercise in "good neighborliness". Officially, the war in Afghanistan did not exist. February 1986 marks a turning point in the official portrayal of the war. Gorbachev, in his address to the CPSU's Twenty-Seventh Congress, characterized the Afghanistan war as a "bleeding wound". Later that year, Shevardnadze referred to the Soviet intervention in Afghanistan as a "sin". . . .

The Afghanistan war changed the Soviet leaders' perceptions about the efficacy of employing troops to suppress non-Russian secessionist movements. It accentuated ethnic strife within the army, especially the resentment of Asian nationalities towards their being used to suppress their ethnic kin in Afghanistan. As a result, Soviet leaders no longer considered their army to be reliable for suppressing secessionist movements.

Demilitarizing Soviet Society

In the Soviet Union the security forces, particularly the army, were key players in domestic politics. Due to its heroic role in

World War II the Soviet army was a cherished institution. It was a microcosm of the Soviet society, drawing soldiers from diverse nationalities. The army was viewed as the main defender of communism, a key function in an ideologically-charged society. Importantly, it was the glue that held together diverse ethnic groups, primarily because it was perceived as being invincible. The army's poor performance in Afghanistan was therefore shocking for soldiers, generals, party cadres, and ordinary citizens. Since the military was an important pillar of the anti-*perestroika* camp, the reverses in Afghanistan weakened anti-reformists, hastened *perestroika*, and facilitated the collapse of the system.

Since a major focus of *perestroika* and *glasnost* was the demilitarization of Soviet society, the war emerged as a rallying point against the military. The poor performance of the Soviet army in Afghanistan and the large number of Soviet casualties fuelled demands to change the military's role. Responding to such pressures, some generals reluctantly accepted a part of the collective guilt. For instance, in mid-1988, Major General [Kim] Tsagolov admitted that "we became the victims of our own illusions". The March 1989 elections to the Supreme Soviet demonstrated the diminished clout of the army; some high ranking officers failed to get elected while some of their radical critics were elected. . . .

Many Soviet Soldiers in Afghanistan Experienced a Moral Crisis

These developments adversely affected the army. In late 1989, a poll conducted by the Soviet Ministry of Defence reported a crisis-like environment and unhappiness among army officers. Importantly, as this news was leaked to civilian newspapers, the internal weakness of the army became public knowledge, thereby strengthening the public's perceptions of the army's weakness.

The Afghanistan war was very harsh for the army. Living conditions for troops were poor. Soldiers were involved in guerrilla warfare in unfamiliar and hostile terrains. They faced constant frictions with Afghan civilians who often supported the

Mujaheddin. Eventually, these conditions contributed to soldiers' lost sense of purpose. Some soldiers observed:

> [The] widespread corruption and smuggling of army equipment for trade in drugs and goods was permitted. And looting among the Afghan population, killing of non-combatants, punitive attacks on villages, as well as torture of prisoners of war was often permitted and even encouraged by officers.

And, in a typical confession which appeared in the press in 1989, one soldier noted:

> There were things we're ashamed to remember. . . . I'm terrified at the thought that if we write a dishonest book about the Afghan war, reading it our children would perhaps want to fight somewhere else. . . . Who are we Afghan war vets? Internationalists or people who messed up someone else's life?

The army was especially brutal towards women and children. In 1987, *Helsinki Watch Reports* reported that the "Russians systematically entered all the houses, executing the inhabitants including women and children often by shooting them in the head". With such reports of looting and brutal treatment of Afghan civilians coming in, the army began losing its moral high ground among Soviet citizens. Another soldier observed:

> We were struck by our own cruelty in Afghanistan. We executed innocent peasants. If one of ours was killed or wounded we would kill women, children and old people as revenge. We killed everything, even the animals.

Some soldiers compared their roles in Afghanistan to that of the Nazi army in World War II. In an interview in 1990, one soldier told *Moscow News* that:

> We were supposedly equated with the participants in the Great Patriotic War, but they defended their homeland, while what did we do? We played the role of the Germans.

In 2011, a man places flowers at a memorial to the fallen soldiers of the Afghanistan war in Kiev, Ukraine. The people of the former Soviet Union and its republics continue to feel the effects of the botched occupation of Afghanistan. © Sergei Starostenko/Xinhua Press/Corbis.

The Plight of Soviet Veterans of the Occupation

Like any other war, the Afghanistan war crippled and injured soldiers who then had to be sent home. Many *Afgantsy* returned from this war desiring to actively participate in the reorganization of society. By the mid-1980s, there were already about a million *Afgantsy* in the Soviet Union and they had emerged "as a new social force in their own right" [as reported in *U.S. News & World Report*].

In the early years of the war, the Soviet leadership, wanting to play down Soviet involvement in Afghanistan, did not acknowledge the presence of the *Afgantsy*. The official media ignored them as well. The *Afgantsy* often could not find jobs. Worse still, military authorities provided them with little assistance in obtaining housing and medical care. Many Soviet citizens also had mixed emotions about them; though the *Afgantsy* had fought for the country, they had fought an unpopular war and had committed atrocities on Afghan civilians. As we have previously noted, some Asian republics (specifically, Tajikistan and Uzbekistan) had ethnic and religious links with Afghans. . . .

Eroding the Legitimacy of the Soviet System

The Soviet Union was an extremely heterogenous country encompassing diverse nationalities and religions. Many of these groups had histories of warring on each other and with Moscow/ St. Petersburg. Though the Soviet system was supposed to be race-blind, it was not so. The non-Russian minorities, Asian as well as European, resented the Russian "capture" of the system. The Afghanistan war accentuated such resentments, since the non-Russian Soviet republics perceived it as a Russian war fought by non-Russian soldiers. Moreover, they noticed the similarities between the Russian oppression of Afghanistan and of the non-Russian Soviet republics. The war therefore seriously eroded the legitimacy of the Soviet system and encouraged secession by the non-Russian republics. It alienated both elites and masses and gave the secessionist movements a popular rallying cause against Russian domination.

Afghanistan consists of three major ethnic groups: Pashtuns, Tajiks, and Uzbeks. Since Tajiks and Uzbeks were also present in the Soviet Union, there was significant unrest in the Asian Soviet republics about the war against people of the same ethnicity. Moreover, the war was perceived by these republics as a Russian war being fought by Central Asians against other Central Asians; [as quoted in an article by Sallie Wise in *Radio Liberty Research*] "our boys are dying for an alien cause." In Tajikistan, the *mullahs* publicly opposed the war, claiming that the Soviets were trying to convert the Afghans into *kafirs* [infidels]. . . .

The Afghanistan war accentuated the cleavages between the non-Russian republics and the Soviet state. It provided a common rallying banner for the secessionist movements and led to many anti-war demonstrations. In effect, it severely eroded the legitimacy of the Soviet system in the eyes of the non-Russian nationalities.

The *Glasnost* Effects on Soviet Governance

The impact of the Afghanistan war was so devastating that war reports challenging the official versions could not be suppressed. Importantly, though not surprisingly, the official media also began showing signs of independence in its war reporting, thereby transforming itself from an outlet for official stories to a barometer of public opinion. Contrary to popular perceptions, we find that *glasnost* did not mark the emergence of a relatively free press in the Soviet Union; *glasnost* only accelerated processes initiated earlier. And the Afghanistan war added new vigour to the forces unleashed by *glasnost*. . . .

The Afghanistan war provided the supporters of *glasnost* and *perestroika* with a key opportunity for redefining the relationship between the citizens and the Soviet state as well as among the various organs of the state itself. As Sergei Lukyanchikov, who directed *Pain*, a documentary on Afghanistan, put it: "The War changed our psychology. It helped *perestroika*".

The Afghan War Was More Damaging to the Soviet Union than the Cold War

The disintegration of the Soviet empire started toward the end of the 1980s when Eastern Europe left the Soviet bloc. The Cold War ended in 1989, and in 1991, the Soviet Union itself disintegrated. This collapse of this particular great power was unexpected in its timing, magnitude, and speed. The existing explanations attribute this collapse to leadership and/or systemic factors. The contributions of the Afghanistan war have been under-emphasized, if not altogether ignored. We have argued that the Afghanistan war was a significant factor leading to the breakdown of the Soviet Union. Further, to answer the two puzzles raised [earlier]—why did the collapse take place only towards the end of the 1980s, and why did the Soviet leaders not employ the army to suppress the secessionist movements— a better appreciation of the impact of the Afghanistan war on Soviet politics is required.

That the Afghanistan war was critical in the collapse of the Soviet Union resonates well with theories emphasizing major wars as key factors in the demise of empires. Major wars among great powers reorient the domestic politics of the warring parties by weakening powerful groups and enfranchising less powerful groups. As the hitherto less powerful become more assertive, the domestic socio-political equilibrium gets disturbed, often irreversibly leading to the collapse of empires. However, are such major wars possible in a world where the great powers possess nuclear weapons? If not, then will major wars no longer remain a key cause of empire breakdowns? Or, do we have to redefine major wars in terms of their implications for domestic politics, and not in terms of the characteristics of the participating actors or the scope of the war? While the Afghanistan war may not be categorized as a major war involving a direct and wide-scale clash of great powers, it was certainly a major war in terms of impacting Soviet domestic politics. Hence, we interpret the key contribution of the Afghanistan war in the collapse of the Soviet Union as only an overlooked case, and not as an exception to those theories that highlight the role of major wars in the demise of empires. . . .

Should the Cold War itself be considered as the major war that led to the collapse of the Soviet Union, as some American commentators in particular seem to believe? In our view—no. In many ways the Cold War is probably better viewed as a chronic problem that was troublesome rather than threatening to the integrity of the USSR. No doubt it imposed a cost on the Soviet system in the form of an ongoing arms race. Some would even argue that it was the fear of those costs rising in the 1980s that first forced the USSR to the negotiating table and then to contemplate the reforms that ultimately led to its disintegration. But showing that the Cold War was costly is one thing: demonstrating an unambiguous empirical relationship between this and the collapse of the Soviet Union is something else altogether. This might make it easier to justify the 40-year policy of military containment. But it does not necessarily make for good history. Indeed, in our view, the Soviet Union—in spite of its multiple inefficiencies—was not only able to bear the costs of the Cold War but had to a large degree internalized them. In the last analysis, it is only dramatic and significant events that cause empires to collapse, not ongoing standoffs—and the only event that fits this bill is the Afghan war, perhaps one of the most over-studied but underestimated military conflicts in the history of the twentieth century; one that analysts of the end of the Cold War continue to ignore at their peril.

US Involvement in Afghanistan Yielded Numerous Unforeseen Consequences

David Wildman and Phyllis Bennis

Phyllis Bennis is a noted author and foreign policy analyst specializing in issues involving the Middle East and the United Nations. David Wildman is the executive secretary for human rights and racial justice with the United Methodist Church's General Board of Global Ministries. In the following viewpoint, the authors assert that the United States has consistently bent Afghan domestic policies away from the interests of women. Early US military aid was furnished with little concern for the alarming philosophical motivations of the mujahideen recipients, Bennis and Wildman maintain. The authors contend that when the Taliban rose to power and drastically stripped women of their rights, the United States willingly recognized this government and continued to support resistance groups led by warlords notorious for brutal attacks against women. Ongoing US military operations have bolstered support for the Taliban and other insurgent groups, the authors argue, thus assuring little progress for women in the immediate future.

Throughout the sequence of empires that have risen and fallen in the region, the land that is now Afghanistan, a nation-

From *Ending the US War in Afghanistan*, published by Olive Branch Press, an imprint of Interlink Publishing Group, Inc. Text copyright © David Wildman and Phyllis Bennis, 2010. Reprinted by permission.

state since the middle of the eighteenth century, has always been prized for its strategic location. In modern history Britain played the key imperial role. In 1893, after years of failed British efforts to win control of Afghanistan, the foreign minister in the colonial government in India, Sir Mortimer Durand, negotiated with the amir of Afghanistan to set the border dividing Afghanistan and what was then British India (today the northwest areas of Pakistan).The Durand Line split the Pashtun territory that still straddles the Afghanistan—Pakistan border, with large Pashtun populations on both sides.

Anti-Communist Action Aids Fundamentalist Islam

The US was not directly involved in Afghanistan until the Cold War. In 1973 Afghanistan's monarchy was overthrown, and a republic declared. A left-wing rebellion in 1978 resulted in the creation of the Democratic Republic of Afghanistan, led by the People's Democratic Party of Afghanistan (PDPA). The PDPA was a communist party whose program tended toward liberal, secular, and socialist reforms, building on some of the social reforms (including outlawing the purdah, a form of isolating women from social contact) that had started in Afghanistan in the 1950s. Although much of the reformist social agenda did not reach beyond Kabul, land reform and support for farmers in the rural areas were high on the PDPA agenda. At least in the cities, Afghan women played a major role in the emerging political and economic life of the country. Kabul quickly developed ties with the Soviet Union, and so, for the US, Afghanistan was now a Cold War target.

President Jimmy Carter's national security advisor, Zbigniew Brzezinski, began a secret campaign of arming, training, and funding Islamist guerrillas known as the Mujahideen against the government in Afghanistan, funneling arms and US and Saudi money through Pakistan's intelligence agency, the ISI. One of the Mujahideen leaders was the young Osama bin Laden, whose organization trained and funded the ISI- and US-backed Mujahideen.

For Washington, consolidating a relationship with Pakistan during the Cold War was important because of Pakistan's hostility to India, which maintained longstanding ties to the Soviet Union. Even more important, undermining the Afghan government would weaken Soviet influence in the region.

In response to growing instability in Afghanistan, on Christmas Eve 1979, the Soviet Union sent in troops, who entered Kabul the following day. Soviet troops would remain in Afghanistan for the next ten years. Defenders of US support for the anti-government and anti-Soviet Mujahideen claimed the US was only helping Afghanistan fight against Soviet occupation. But in 1998 Brzezinski admitted:

> According to the official version of history, CIA aid to the mujahideen began in 1980, that is to say, after the Soviet Union invaded Afghanistan, 24 December 1979. But the reality, secretly guarded until now, is completely otherwise. Indeed, it was July 3, 1979, that President Carter signed the first directive for secret aid to the opponents of the pro-Soviet regime in Kabul. And that very day, I wrote a note to the president in which I explained to him that in my opinion, this aid was going to induce a Soviet military intervention. . . . We didn't push the Russians to intervene, but we knowingly increased the probability that they would.

The presence of the Soviet troops gave rise to what the journalist Steve Coll described as "fluid networks of stateless Islamic radicals whose global revival after 1979 eventually birthed bin Laden's al Qaeda." In 1998 Brzezinski dismissed the consequences of the US backing Islamist extremists: "What is most important to the history of the world?" he asked. "The Taliban or the collapse of the Soviet empire? Some stirred-up Moslems or the liberation of Central Europe and the end of the cold war?"

Rebel leader Gulbuddin Hekmatyar answers journalists' questions in Sekhva, Afghanistan, in 1992. Hekmatyar was supported by the United States in the conflict against the Soviet Union, but he later became committed to a radical brand of Islam. © AP Images/Heidi Bradner.

The Escalation of the Civil War

Afghanistan became the centerpiece of Ronald Reagan's doc-
trine of active military backing for anti-Soviet resistance groups.
Throughout his eight years in office Reagan escalated support for
the Mujahideen, thereby consolidating relations with Pakistan
and Saudi Arabia as bulwarks against pro-Soviet India. In 1985
Reagan's CIA director, William Casey, crafted National Security
Decision Directive 166, which provided the legal justification for
a huge escalation of the CIA's role inside Afghanistan. During
that time the Reagan administration also became special patrons
of Gulbuddin Hekmatyar, head of one of the most powerful and
most extreme Islamist guerrilla organizations. Hekmatyar had
the closest ties to the ISI, received most of the funds from the US
and the Saudis, and was the main recipient of the much-coveted
Stinger anti-aircraft missiles provided by the US. He was one of
the Mujahideen leaders brought to a highly publicized White
House visit in 1985, where President Reagan welcomed the
Islamist guerrillas as the "moral equivalent of America's founding fathers."

From 1985 on, the US- and Pakistan-backed Islamist guerrillas escalated the fight against the Soviet forces in Afghanistan.
The violence forced almost all the population of the country
from their homes, and millions fled Afghanistan to seek refuge
in neighboring Iran or especially Pakistan, where the United
Nations scrambled to put together survival camps for the flood
of refugees.

When the Soviet troops were forced out of Afghanistan in
1988–1989, the civil war escalated, as the Mujahideen organizations continued to challenge the government in Kabul. In 1991
the US and the Soviet Union agreed to end military aid to both
sides, and within a year the Mujahideen organizations overthrew
the government. The Democratic Republic of Afghanistan was
over. Its president, Najibullah, was arrested and publicly tortured
to death. The still well-armed Mujahideen turned on each other,
and fighting among them, ethnically based and otherwise, con-

tinued. Where the Islamist factions consolidated power, they imposed repressive social laws, based on extremist interpretations of Islamic law, or sharia. Women paid the heaviest price under the harsh laws, which overturned the fragile gains women (at least urban women) had made since 1978, and aimed instead to exclude them from most social, national, political, and economic life, and bring them under the full control of their fathers and husbands.

In 1993 the warring factions agreed on a government, with Burhanuddin Rabbani, a Tajik leader, proclaimed president, and Hekmatyar, a Pashtun, named prime minister. But the quarreling coalition of Islamists continued fighting. Civilian casualties continued to mount. Within a year a new Pashtun-dominated group within the array of jockeying factions took the lead in challenging Rabbani's government. It was called the Taliban.

The Taliban Gains Popular Support

The Taliban (or "students") organization was made up primarily of young Pashtun men whose parents had fled Afghanistan during the anti-Soviet and civil wars, and who had mostly grown up in the crowded, squalid refugee camps in Pakistan. They grew up impoverished, disempowered, angry, without jobs, and without hope. Most of their education, if indeed they had access to education at all, was provided by Saudi-funded and Pakistani-run madrassas, or Islamic schools, many of which taught a severe, extremist interpretation of the Qur'an and Islamic law.

In 1996 the Taliban captured control of Kabul. Rabbani's government collapsed. Some government officials fled Afghanistan, seeking refuge in countries that had long supported them from outside, including Pakistan. Others, including Rabbani himself, remained in the country, but headed north to join the shaky coalition of anti-Taliban Islamist guerrillas known as the Northern Alliance. As the Pakistan-backed Taliban had gained power, Pakistan's competitor India had emerged as a key supporter of the Northern Alliance. So with the Cold War over, the

US turning its attention elsewhere, and the Soviet Union about to collapse, the Afghan civil war players took on regional sponsors to replace their global backers. Pakistan escalated its support for the newly empowered Taliban, while Indian interests (and soon the CIA) became inextricably linked to the Northern Alliance.

As the Taliban consolidated its control over Kabul and the countryside, it quickly introduced even more extreme versions of sharia, in which many women were virtually imprisoned in their homes. Harsh punishments, including stoning to death and amputations, escalated. But the Taliban also knew how to win the loyalty of the local population, war-weary and exhausted from the years of fighting. The Taliban had promised to put an end to the fighting among the militias that had led to so much death and destruction for Afghan civilians. As a result, in many parts of the country, the Taliban was welcomed, and won some level of popular support with the expectation that its ascension to power would lead to some break in the fighting, some hope for stability. The Taliban were not corrupt, in stark contrast to many of the Western-armed tribal and ethnic bosses they fought against. (In fact, Taliban leader Mullah Omar famously lived in a primitive hut, eschewing the luxuries of other powerful leaders.) So people did not have to pay bribes to deal with local officials, and the Taliban's campaigns to end petty crime and corruption brought them more support.

The Civil War Continues

Internationally, the Taliban government in Kabul was recognized only by Pakistan, Saudi Arabia, and the United Arab Emirates. Other countries continued to recognize the deposed Burhanuddin Rabbani, now one of the leaders of the Northern Alliance, as the legitimate president. The Northern Alliance, led by Rabbani and the popular Islamist leader and defense minister Ahmad Shah Massoud, continued fighting against the Taliban, and the US supported them.

In February and May 1998, two massive earthquakes killed thousands of Afghans. In August, al-Qaeda was held responsible for the bombings of US embassies in Kenya and Tanzania. Two weeks later, the US launched retaliatory missile strikes against Afghanistan, targeting what were supposed to be al-Qaeda bases there. President [Bill] Clinton said, "Our mission was clear—to strike at the network of radical groups affiliated with, and funded by, Osama bin Laden, the pre-eminent organizer and financier of international terrorism in the world today." But bin Laden was nowhere to be found by those strikes, although dozens of Afghans were killed and injured. By 1999 the US had pressured the United Nations to impose harsh sanctions on Afghanistan, ostensibly to force the Taliban to extradite bin Laden for trial in the US.

In the meantime the civil war continued. The Northern Alliance, still led by Ahmad Shah Masood, kept up the effort to depose the Taliban, although the competing opposition leaders had splintered into factions also at war against each other. International opposition to the Taliban rose, particularly in response to their destruction of the sixth-century Buddhist statues carved into cliff sides in Bamiyan, carried out in 1998 between the two earthquakes. The US also publicly attacked the Taliban for their oppression of women—while ignoring a very similar pattern of attacks on women by the warlords of the US-backed Northern Alliance and the rest of the Islamist guerrilla opposition.

But in fact, public expressions of outrage aside, as soon as the Taliban seized power the US was quite willing to deal with them strategically despite their brutality, attacks on women, and other human rights violations. Afghanistan was still located in a strategic neighborhood, regardless of who was in power in Kabul. Oil and gas pipelines were still on the agenda. The US-based Unocal oil company wanted to meet with the Taliban. So on October 7, 1996, just after the Taliban had seized control of Kabul, Afghan-American neoconservative and Reagan administration insider

© 2009 by Aislin and Cagle Cartoons, Inc.

Zalmay Khalilzad, who then worked for Unocal, wrote in the *Washington Post* that it was "time for the United States to re-engage" with the Taliban. At the same time, as the Taliban consolidated their rule and Afghan women were being forced out of public life, Khalilzad coordinated the visit of top Taliban officials to the United States. The *Post* found him "at a luxury Houston hotel . . . chatting pleasantly over dinner with leaders of Afghanistan's Taliban regime about their shared enthusiasm for a proposed multibillion-dollar pipeline deal."

A few years later, after the US invaded Afghanistan to overthrow Khalilzad's dining companions, the respected *World Press Review* would note that the "United States was slow to condemn the Taliban in the mid-1990s because the Taliban seemed to favor US oil company Unocal to build two pipelines across Afghanistan."

US Occupation Bolsters Taliban Support

The internecine battles among Afghan militias continued, even with the Taliban defeated and the US-backed Afghan government of President Hamid Karzai installed in power since 2002. One of the most extremist leaders of the anti-Soviet Mujahideen guerrillas, Gulbuddin Hekmatyar—the one who had been provided with hundreds of millions of dollars from the CIA and welcomed to the White House as a "freedom fighter" by President Reagan back in the 1980s despite being known for throwing acid in the faces of unveiled women in his university days—had fought against the Taliban since they took over in 1996. But then he turned against the US-led occupation, pledging to kill American troops just as he had once killed Soviets. In 2006 he announced his allegiance to Osama bin Laden.

But the Taliban's opposition to the US emerged only after the US invasion, and focused on getting the US out of Afghanistan. In fact, US officials recognize that the Taliban's danger to the US, if any, was limited to their providing refuge for al-Qaeda; on their own the Taliban was no threat to the US (except to US troops occupying their country).

Indeed, by the middle of 2007, when the Taliban resurgence in Afghanistan was well underway, many US officials still claimed they had no idea how the resurgence could have happened. The *New York Times* reported that, since the quick overthrow of the Taliban government in 2001,

> American intelligence agencies had reported that the Taliban were so decimated they no longer posed a threat, according to two senior intelligence officials who reviewed the reports. The American sense of victory had been so robust that the top C.I.A. specialists and elite Special Forces units who had helped liberate Afghanistan had long since moved on to the next war, in Iraq. When it came to reconstruction, big goals were

announced, big projects identified. Yet in the year Mr. [George W.] Bush promised a "Marshall Plan" for Afghanistan, the country received less assistance per capita than did post-conflict Bosnia and Kosovo, or even desperately poor Haiti, according to a RAND Corporation study. Washington has spent an average of $3.4 billion a year reconstructing Afghanistan, less than half of what it has spent in Iraq, according to the Congressional Research Service.

One respondent summarized the view of many rural communities, "the presence of the Taliban is a blessing for the US as it is an excuse for the US to be here, otherwise other countries would all ask the US to leave the region. So the Taliban legitimizes the US presence." Why should anyone have been surprised that the Taliban were resurgent, still challenging the US, years after they were driven out of Kabul in 2001?

The Taliban resurgence beginning in 2008 was linked directly to the more active combat initiated by the US and NATO forces in Afghanistan. Despite significant opposition by many in the Afghan public, the Taliban remained a viable part of the country's mélange of ethnic, tribal, and Islamist militias.

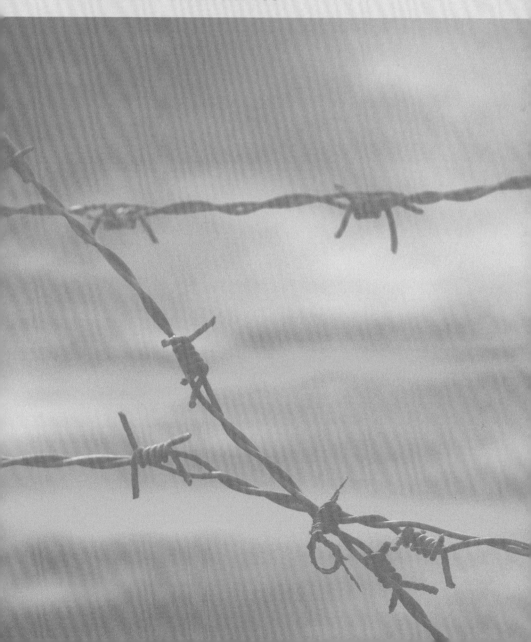

CHAPTER 3

Personal Narratives

Chapter Exercises

1. ## Writing Prompt

   Imagine you are an Afghan teenager living during the Soviet occupation. Write a one-page journal entry about your daily life.

2. ## Group Activity

   Break into groups and compose five interview questions that would be useful if you were collecting oral histories from Soviet soldiers deployed to Afghanistan. Remember that both men and women served in the Soviet army.

Life for Afghans in a War Zone

Niyaz Turdi, as told to Alex Klaits and Gulchin Gulmamadova-Klaits

Alex Klaits and Gulchin Gulmamadova-Klaits have worked for a variety of international aid organizations in Afghanistan, Tajikistan, and Kyrgyzstan. Their book Love and War in Afghanistan *includes stories they gathered while travelling in the northeastern provinces of Afghanistan in 2004. In the following viewpoint, the authors interview Niyaz Turdi, an Afghan Turkmen. Turdi recalls the morning of his 1980 wedding when his village was attacked by Russian helicopters. The attack injured most of his family members, killed his brother, and left his mother with fatal injuries. He recounts the complete destruction of a neighboring village by tanks and assault helicopters, illustrating the ferocity of Soviet operations.*

I was nineteen years old in 1980 when my father decided that it was time for me to get married. My female relatives assured me that my bride, Amina, was a beautiful young girl. She was from the neighboring village of Chargul Teppa and had already learned the basics of carpet weaving from her mother. Thanks to her skills, she fetched a fairly high bride price. My father had saved up funds for several years from our harvest and carpet

Niyaz Turdi, as told to Alex Klaits and Gulchin Gulmamadova-Klaits, *Love and War in Afghanistan*. New York: Seven Stories Press, 2005, pp. 69–73, 75–76. Copyright © 2005 by Seven Stories Press. All rights reserved. Reproduced by permission.

sales to afford her. He told me that she was like an investment for the future. "Right now, she doesn't have a great deal of skill in weaving, but if she practices with your mother for a few years, she'll be able to bring in a lot of cash for you later on."

Making Wedding Preparations

The day before my wedding, dozens of my relatives and neighbors had gathered in our village for the celebration. Our small house was abuzz with activity. The women busily cleaned the house, baked more bread than I'd ever seen before, and cleaned a mountain of rice for the pilaf. My mother and three sisters were also putting the finishing touches on some gifts for Amina's family; they had woven a couple of carpets and sewn beautiful dresses for her and her sisters, which they placed inside ornate metal trunks. Some of the men went to the market to buy all kinds of things for the next day, while a few others rounded up the sheep they were planning to slaughter for the hundreds of guests. I relaxed in the guest room and drank tea with the other men.

That night I thought about what lay in store for the next day. Among us Turkmen, there's a tradition whereby the new bride will be brought straight from her own kitchen to the groom's house by her relatives on horseback. She's not supposed to be wearing any special wedding clothes on this day, just some outfit that she might wear around the house. This symbolizes that the bride is more concerned with hard work and serving her groom's family than in indulging in frivolous things.

A Raid on the Wedding Party

As I drifted off to sleep, lots of sweet questions swirled in my head: What will I say to Amina when I first see her? What will she look like? Is she as beautiful as my relatives promise? But my dreams were anything but sweet. As dawn approached, I had a terrible nightmare that Soviet helicopters were circling above our village, laying waste to everything in their path. My fellow villagers were screaming and begging me to run for cover. . . .

The dream blended quickly into reality. The next thing I knew I was thrown several feet into the air when a Soviet missile struck the mosque next door. I immediately scrambled to my feet and stumbled out into our courtyard. It had just become light outside. And just as I exited the house, a missile landed right next to our kitchen. The bomb didn't cause much damage, but it burrowed so deeply that water from an underground source was sent spouting into the air.

I looked up and saw that there were three or four helicopters circling above our village. Another bomb struck right behind our house, and a few seconds later a third bomb landed on a house a couple of doors away. There was total chaos as my relatives all ran in different directions. Most of them ran out of the house on to the street, shrieking with terror. But I just stood in place watching the helicopters above. Why would it be any safer out on the street or in another house? I thought. Bombs are exploding all over our village. There had been a few raids on our village over the course of the past year but nothing approaching the ferocity of this attack. Why today? I asked myself. Why on my wedding day? Then it occurred to me that some of the guests at the wedding party were actually mujahedin insurgents. So maybe this isn't a coincidence after all, I thought.

A Bomb Strikes the Family

As these disconnected ideas were spinning around in my head, a helicopter swooped down maybe one hundred yards away from our house and hung in the air, as though the pilot was sizing up the wisdom of an attack. Instinctively, I ran back inside the house to hide. It turned out that I was suddenly all alone in one section of the house. Most of our guests had fled, but I knew that some of my family members were probably huddled in a room directly across the courtyard from me. I had often hidden in that room with my family during past bombing raids.

As I dashed into the empty room, I looked out the window, whose glass had been shattered, to see whether the helicopter had finally moved on. But just at that moment, it fired a missile directly at the room where my family was gathered. I was blinded by the light of the explosion. The thing that I remember most vividly was how our strong, wooden roof beams had splintered into tiny pieces. Then I heard the screams from all the people who had sought shelter in that room. Even with the helicopter still circling above, I rushed across our courtyard to see if I could do anything to help the survivors.

The force of the bomb was so great that there was very little left of the room. At first, I couldn't even see my relatives—there was thick dust everywhere. I had to shut my eyes to shield them from the debris in the air. The only way I was able to find my way to the victims was by listening for their cries. "Please, somebody help me!" I heard one of my sisters wailing. When I finally groped my way across the room, I found her with a large gash on her head and a badly injured shoulder. As almost all of the people in the room, she was nearly naked as her clothes had been shredded by the explosion. Then I heard another relative crying for assistance.

Many Villagers Suffered Injuries

It wasn't until the dust settled that I could assess the damage. One of my sisters had somehow completely escaped injury, but the remaining eight people in the room, including my parents, were badly wounded and drenched in blood. A couple of my family members had serious injuries on their legs and feet, while others had large chunks of skin torn away. Almost all them had pieces of the smashed timber roof beams lodged in their bodies. My one and only brother, who was five years younger than I, was the only fatality.

Our possessions were strewn in every direction, and a couple of the metal trunks, which were intended for Amina's family, had been thrown clear over our house's surrounding wall. I had to run around the house collecting clothing so that my female relatives could cover themselves.

The bombs exploded around our village for another half hour or so. But it felt like an eternity. When the helicopters finally left us in peace, we took all of our wounded family members to a neighbor who was a doctor. When we arrived, a large number of wounded people—including women and children—were already lying in his courtyard awaiting treatment. The range of injuries was shocking: some had lost arms and legs, others had serious head injuries, and still others had pieces of shrapnel buried in their bodies. The fortunate ones only had light injuries on their hands and feet. There were, in fact, so many injured people from our village that young men were sent out to neighboring villages to summon their doctors for assistance. To this day, there are many people in my native village who still bear the scars from that malicious attack: they walk with limps, are missing limbs, or have big scars on their bodies. In total, sixteen people from our village, including my brother, lost their lives on that awful morning.

The Attack Disrupted All Aspects of Normal Life

When my mother saw how many severely injured people were in need of urgent attention, she turned around and started walking out of the doctor's courtyard. "I just have a small cut on my side," she said to me as we looked at the horrible scene before us. "Why should I waste the doctor's precious time when he has so many other pressing cases?" As a child, my mother had survived a couple of bouts of serious illness without much complaint. My Tajik grandfather nicknamed her Sangina, which means "made of stone." Her friends used to joke that this was a disservice as Allah had actually endowed her with the strength of steel. I urged my mother to stay and have the doctor examine her wound, but she insisted on returning home and mourning her lost son. "Your brother's spirit is still in our house, and I need to be with him," she told me.

As I sat on the ground of the courtyard trying to comfort my injured relatives, the tragedy of the events of that morning really struck me. When I had gone to sleep only a few hours previously, I had been in a house bursting with merriment and joy. But now, it had been transformed into a place of grief and mourning. My family and Amina's family, after consulting the local mullah, agreed that we would delay the wedding party indefinitely, and we would just be considered married. According to our traditions, it's disrespectful to celebrate a wedding party in the year following the death of a close family member. In the two or three weeks after my brother's burial, it hardly even occurred to me that I was in fact a newlywed.

Fatalities Continue to Mount Long After the Attack

As for my mother, she was completely absorbed in the mourning ceremonies for her youngest son. She didn't mention the pain in her side to a single person until one night she started screaming in agony. In all my life, I'd never heard my mother cry in pain. We had no choice but to wake the exhausted doctor so that he could examine her. After a quick examination, he told me that we would need to take her to the Spinzar hospital in Kunduz city so that she could get an x-ray. "There appears to be some metal stuck in her body, but I can't make a better diagnosis than that," he told me. "She'll definitely need better treatment than I could possibly offer."

First thing in the morning, my mother, my sister, one of my cousins, and I caught a taxi into the city, about an hour away. My mother was suffering terribly, but she tried her best not to show it. When we arrived at the hospital, the corridors were flooded with injured people and their relatives. The crying and moaning were nearly overwhelming. After a few hours of examining my mother, the doctors emerged looking dejected. "Your mother has suffered a serious injury," one doctor told me. "A small piece of shrapnel is lodged in her large intestine. We can try to operate, but the surgery is very risky, and we can't guarantee that she'll survive. Everything is in the hands of Allah." We decided to go ahead with the surgery, and a few days later my mother died. . . .

The Complete Destruction of a Village

One afternoon [years later], about twenty tanks and hundreds of Soviet and Afghan troops swept through our village on their way to Qarai Qeshlaq. Then a couple dozen Soviet helicopters passed over us and started carpet bombing Qarai Qeshlaq. For about an hour, the ground shook as if we were at the heart of an earthquake, even though we were a couple of miles away from the village under attack. The Soviets had much better equipment and arsenals than the mujahedin, who could only carry out their guerilla attacks under the cover of darkness. As a mujahedin friend of mine once told me, "The day belongs to the infidels, but the nights belong to us."

Once it finally began to get dark, we saw the Soviet troops and tanks retreat from Qarai Qeshlaq. We waited another hour or so to make sure that they wouldn't return. Then a group of men from our village decided to venture up the road to find out how we might be able to assist the wounded. But shortly after we'd arrived in Qarai Qeshlaq, we realized that our search and rescue mission would be a short one.

I can't begin to describe the complete and utter destruction we witnessed. It was the silence that struck me first—this was a time in the evening when the men are usually on their way home from the mosque, and their voices fill the air. There was not a single house or even a tree still standing. When we entered people's courtyards and barns, there were animal carcasses lying everywhere. And inside the homes, there was nothing but dead bodies lying in pools of blood amid their scattered possessions.

Digging a Mass Grave and Finding a Single Survivor

Our small band was joined by a couple of dozen men from other nearby settlements. We spread out across the village walking from house to house with small kerosene lamps looking for survivors. At one point, my friend and I walked into a house where three women were sitting in their burqas with their legs covered by blankets. If these women were in fact alive, we didn't want to compromise their modesty by barging in on them. So we went back outside and called an older man from our village to investigate. It turned out that they had been shot, and their dead bodies were left leaning up against the walls.

After discussing what we should do, we decided to dig several long shallow trenches in the ground at the edge of the village to serve as mass graves. Then we began to carry the victims one by one across the village to the mass grave. Within a few minutes, I was completely covered in blood. It took us the whole night to gather the corpses together in their final resting place.

But as the first light of dawn shone, a miracle occurred. One of the men from our village appeared holding the hand of the lone survivor from Qarai Qeshlaq—a young boy who had been using the bathroom when the Soviets launched their attack. He had jumped down into the pit, which was half filled with excrement, thus avoiding detection. The child was still in shock. He didn't say a word to any of us. He only nodded or shook his head to answer our questions.

The boy was the only lucky one. Every other living thing in Qarai Qeshlaq—more than 450 people and all the animals— were shot dead. The village was soon resettled by new residents who wanted to take advantage of the rich agriculture in the area. But before the new people arrived in the village, it was renamed Qatli Om, which means "Murdered en Masse."

Mother of Three Reflects on Work in Afghanistan

Jan Cartwright

Jan Cartwright is a writer for FrontLines, *a US Agency for International Development (USAID) publication. In the following viewpoint, Cartwright discusses US Foreign Service Officer Sarah-Ann Lynch's experience working in Afghanistan. Lynch says the most difficult thing about travelling to Afghanistan was making the decision to leave behind her three children. Lynch describes her work in Afghanistan as very fast-paced—she never knew what she would be doing from one day to the next. Lynch believes her work in Afghanistan was part of something very important.*

For Sarah-Ann Lynch, a seasoned Foreign Service Officer and mother of three—ages 15, 12, and 8—the most difficult thing about serving in Afghanistan was making the decision to go. The year-long position would entail an extended separation from her family.

"What I told my kids is that this is a really important effort that I needed to be a part of," she said. "I think they understood and were proud of what I was doing." In July 2008, Lynch arrived in Kabul as the director of the Agency's Afghanistan program

Jan Cartwright, "Mother of Three Reflects on Work in Afghanistan," *USAID FrontLines*, November 2009. USAID.gov.

office. Knowing that the separation would be difficult, the family "tried to treat it as kind of a normal year, maintaining routines as much as possible."

As head of the program office, Lynch was in charge of assembling and managing the team that handled strategy and budget functions for the office, as well as donor coordination, information management, and cross-cutting issues such as gender.

"We had such a committed and solid team, both on the American and Afghan sides—and it's rewarding for me to know that this team that I helped put together is still together, doing great and very important work to improve the lives of Afghans."

The pace and pressure of the work was relentless but invigorating. Within two weeks of arriving, Lynch was asked to give a presentation on all USAID programs in the country to senior Afghan government officials.

"When you went to sleep at night, you never knew what challenges you would face the next day. It was definitely an exciting job," she said.

Lynch was able to get out of Kabul fairly frequently for meetings and project visits. One of her most vivid memories is of a dedication ceremony she attended for a women's garden center in Baghlan province in northern Afghanistan. The project would allow local women to receive training and also have private space to themselves—a rare opportunity for many Afghan women. "I got to sit down with a small group of women at the center.

Like women everywhere, they just want more opportunities for their children and for themselves," said Lynch, who has some insights into the struggles and rewards of motherhood.

While in Afghanistan, Lynch kept in close touch with family back home. "We Skyped, we phoned each other, and we e-mailed, so I kept in lots of communication that way. Plus, employees are allowed four breaks during the year, and I did manage to touch base with my family on all of those breaks, so we had the human contact as well during the year. And I think that really helped a lot, because I did stay connected."

Lynch grew up in Stoughton, Mass., and attended Mount Holyoke College and Tufts University's Fletcher School of Law and Diplomacy. Although she started her career working in international business, she was always drawn to development, having served in the Peace Corps in Morocco.

Lynch has been with USAID for over 16 years and has served in Bangladesh and Peru, but she counts her posting in Afghanistan as her most memorable assignment. It was also the fulfillment of her dream to work in a region that she had studied in graduate school.

"My experience in Afghanistan turned out to be even more enjoyable than I had anticipated . . . we all felt that we were taking part in something very important. It made us want to work hard to make a difference."

Lynch is now based in Washington as director of strategic planning and programs for the Afghanistan-Pakistan Task Force.

Afghanistan War: Lessons from the Soviet War

Edward Girardet

Journalist Edward Girardet has reported from war-torn regions throughout Africa and Asia since the 1970s and is the author of several books on Afghanistan. As a foreign correspondent, he first began covering Afghanistan in 1979, a few months before the Soviet invasion. In the following viewpoint, Girardet relates his experience reporting on the Soviet and the US-led offensives in Afghanistan. He claims that during the Soviet invasion, the media had regular access to ordinary Afghans—a privilege not given to reporters during the US invasion. He asserts that many parallels can be drawn between the two wars, and that the West must show that they are not in Afghanistan to impose their own views but to inspire hope for Afghanistan's future.

It was early summer, 1982. The Soviet war in Afghanistan was gathering momentum against the mujahideen, the country's disparate but increasingly widespread resistance movement. I'd just trekked for 10 days across rugged mountains from neighboring Pakistan to the beleaguered Panjshir Valley, an assertive thorn against the Red Army's might barely 40 miles north of Kabul.

I was traveling with a half-dozen mujahideen guerrillas accompanying a French medical team being sent to replace a group of volunteer doctors working clandestinely among the civilian population.

My purpose was to report on the largest Soviet-led offensive against the mujahideen to that date. More than 12,000 Soviet and Afghan troops would attempt to crush 3,000 fighters led by Ahmed Shah Massoud, known as the "Lion of Panjshir" and one of the 20th century's most effective guerrilla commanders.

Last month's NATO-led operation in Marjah in Helmand Province—the largest offensive of the current war—put me in mind of the Panjshir. There are clear lessons from the nearly decade-long Soviet occupation that the international community might heed in its ninth year of war in Afghanistan, with the biggest battle campaign now under way.

The Panjshir push was roughly the same size as the Marjah offensive—called Operation Moshtarak—and involved 10,000 to 12,000 coalition and Afghan troops. In the Soviet war, Western journalists reported primarily from the guerrilla side. But in contrast to most of today's media, embedded with NATO troops, we had constant access to ordinary Afghans. We walked through the countryside sleeping in villages, with long evenings spent drinking tea and talking with the locals. Frank conversation doesn't happen when one party wears body armor or is flanked by heavily armed soldiers: Afghans will only tell you what they think you want to hear. Or, even more crucial, what suits their own interests. Hence the highly questionable veracity of opinion polls in Afghanistan today.

Similar to the Marjah offensive, the Soviets warned the population of the impending attack with propaganda leaflets and radio broadcasts. They appealed to the Panjshiris to support the government in return for cash and other incentives, such as subsidized wheat. Their tactic was to force the guerrillas out, but allow the civilians to remain. To make their point, the communists lambasted the guerrillas as criminals supported by foreign interests in the tribal areas across the border in Pakistan, a tactic similar to those used by the Americans against the Taliban today.

Approaching the Panjshir that summer of 1982, we skirted the massive Bagram Air Base, today run by the Americans but then a hugely fortified Soviet bastion blistering with helicopter gunships and MiGs. On reaching the outer edges of the mighty Hindu Kush, we encountered groups of refugees hiding among the gorges. Days earlier, Massoud had evacuated the area's 50,000 or more people, somewhat less than the population affected by the Marjah campaign. He did this to minimize civilian casualties and to give his fighters free rein.

Before dawn the morning after we arrived, we could hear the ominous drone of helicopters. As the throbbing grew louder, tiny specks appeared on the horizon, gunships sweeping over the jagged snowcapped peaks like hordes of wasps. Soon the hollow thud of rockets and bombs were pounding guerrilla positions. Intermittently, pairs of MiG-23 jets and the new highly maneuverable SU-24 fighter bombers shrieked across the skies dropping their loads.

With two journalist colleagues, I climbed to a 7,000-foot vantage over the valley. Dozens of front-line guerrillas, looking like Cuban revolutionaries with their long hair and beards, lounged among the rocks in the bright sun watching the spectacle. Grinning, they handed us glasses of tea, oblivious of helicopters roaring barely 500 meters overhead. Massoud's strategy was to empty the valley, let the Soviets in, and have fighters hit the occupation forces in their own time.

It was reminiscent of a 19th-century painting of picnickers casually watching a distant battle. We counted no fewer than 200 helicopter sorties that morning, while scores of tanks and armored personnel carriers ground their way up the riverbed, the only way to penetrate the valley because guerrillas had mined

The Soviet army base in the outskirts of Kabul afforded terrible living conditions for the poorly trained and supplied soldiers. © Romano Cagnoni/Hulton Archive/Getty Images.

the road. Unlike the current anti-NATO insurgency, however, the use of improvised explosive devices was limited; while suicide bombers, a relatively recent tactic introduced by Al Qaeda, were never used by the mujahideen.

There seemed to be many simultaneous operations: Across the valley, M-24 gunships circled like sharks to attack guerrilla positions. Farther on, trucks mounted with rockets fired into mountainsides. Just below, a Soviet machine gun leveled off bursts against guerrillas among the boulders above. Nearby, shirtless Red Army soldiers took breaks sunning on looted carpets spread on the flat roofs of houses, while others redeployed, jogging single file through shrapnel-torn mulberry trees.

The Soviet/Afghan force quickly took the valley, proclaiming victory. The reality was far different. Massoud's experienced guerrillas suffered few casualties and, within days, launched assaults against the entrenched Red Army troops. Afghan government soldiers, too, poorly paid and disheartened, slipped out at night with their weapons to join the resistance.

Massoud eventually made a truce with the Soviets. This enabled the Red Army a "take and hold" policy with several garrisons in the Panjshir. Some civilians returned, while the guerrillas established their own concealed bases in mountains beyond. The truce was much criticized by rival groups of mujahideen, but it was part of a long-term strategy: Massoud had no intention of collaborating with the regime. Occupation troops first had to leave before any unity government could be formed. It's the same refrain today by the Taliban, Hezb-e-Islami Gulbuddin, and other opposition groups.

For years, Massoud kept the Soviets tied down while focusing on other areas and building a highly proficient regional force denying the communists swaths of countryside. The mujahideen—like the Taliban now—always felt they had time on their side. All they needed to do was wear down the Red Army. At the height of the occupation, the Soviets commanded 120,000 troops in Afghanistan, compared with the 150,000 coalition high expected by next fall with completion of the US troop surge. When the Soviets, who suffered at least 15,000 deaths and thousands of injured, pulled out in February 1989, they had little to show but widespread destruction of much of the country. Three years later, the Moscow-backed regime in Kabul crumbled. Today, it's as if the Soviets had never been there.

Unlike NATO forces, who now make pointed efforts to protect civilians, the Soviets and their Afghan cohorts often deliberately targeted local populations. Throughout its war, however, the Red Army held little more than the main towns. The countryside remained largely in the hands of the mujahideen. Similarly, today, 70 percent of the country is ranked as "insecure" by the United Nations.

The parallels of the panjshir with today just keep rolling. Today's insurgents fight much like the mujahideen; and, in fact, many now call themselves mujahideen. Many commanders earned their battle spurs during the Soviet war. Their fighters hide among the locals and, often, are the locals. If things get tough, they deploy elsewhere.

Like Marjah, a deliberate joint NATO-Afghan operation, the Soviets made a point of involving Afghan partners and constantly extolled the effectiveness of the Kabul regime in the hope that Afghan security forces would assume the brunt of the war. In reality, the Soviets were running the show just as US, British, and other forces are today.

Ironically, the Soviets did succeed in creating an effective Afghan fighting force. Following the Red Army withdrawal, the communists fought hard and well against fundamentalist mujahideen supported by the Pakistani military in eastern Afghanistan. The communist regime finally fell for political, not military, reasons. There's little doubt that Afghan security capabilities can be improved today, but can the Kabul regime achieve acceptance?

Red Army commanders were very aware that they couldn't trust "their" Afghans. Massoud's mujahideen enjoyed full details of planned operations before launch. Many government, military, and police officials, including senior commanders, secretly collaborated with the resistance, just as pro-Taliban and other insurgent collaborators have infiltrated most ministries of the current administration.

The Soviets also succeeded in building a highly effective network of informers and often thwarted resistance operations based on this intelligence. But they never gained the upper hand. The more effective guerrilla commanders always seemed to keep two steps ahead of the game. (Twice, while reporting for the Monitor during the 1980s, I was nearly captured by Soviet heliborne troops after being informed upon by local Afghans.)

Moscow's attempts to establish hard-core militia fronts by purchasing their allegiance also faltered. The old adage of "you can only rent an Afghan, you can never buy him" remained the rule of thumb. Many militia had "just in case" arrangements with the mujahideen, just as today numerous police and military units collaborating with NATO forces have their own deals with the insurgents.

While the coalition may claim the Marjah offensive routed the Taliban, it will probably have little impact on the long-term fighting capability of the opposition, even if NATO holds terrain captured.

To claim success shows a poor understanding of Afghanistan. Only a small proportion of the insurgents are actually fighting. The majority of sympathizers will have buried their weapons or simply blended in among the civilians. Others are in the process of deploying elsewhere, just as Massoud used the interim to organize fighting fronts throughout the north. There's no way that all these areas can be controlled militarily.

Many of the Western governments operating in Afghanistan focus on their own zones, such as the Dutch in Uzurugan and the Germans in Kunduz. Most officers come for six-month deployments, a period in which no one can even begin to understand this country. It is this lack of understanding about Afghan culture and thought that is the biggest problem today. Crucial, too, is the need for a long-term approach for the next 30 years. Talk of exit strategy only plays into the hands of insurgents biding their time.

The Western missions, barricaded in Kabul compounds, are out of touch with what's happening on the ground. So are their intelligence operations. They spend billions on recovery or security initiatives, yet are reluctant to invest in credible information efforts.

As the Marjah operation demonstrates, there is still the belief that the problem can be resolved by clearing out the insurgents militarily, and holding the territory while installing new top-down structures—"a government in a box."

For most Afghans I've talked to on recent trips to Kabul and eastern, central, and southern Afghanistan, justice, not security, is the principal concern. Even where the military is in control,

Afghans slip out to Taliban-controlled areas to seek fair dealing, having more confidence in Taliban sharia courts than in Karzai-regime judges. They see lack of rule of law and international community failure to develop a functioning economy, particularly in the countryside where 80 percent of Afghans live. And they increasingly perceive the coalition as a foreign occupation force, much like the Soviets.

The Soviets thought they could subdue Afghanistan through brute force, political indoctrination, and bribes. They wanted to put across the notion that their form of government had far more to offer than the jihad embraced by the mujahideen. They lost.

The West, following dangerously close to the path of its Soviet predecessor in Afghanistan, must show that it isn't there to impose its own views but to help ordinary people feel they have a future.

Afghanistan's Last Two Jews Feuding

Steven Gutkin

Steven Gutkin is a contributor to AP Online. In the following viewpoint, Gutkin describes the feud between the last two Jews still living in Afghanistan in 2002. Although Afghanistan once had a thriving Jewish community, only two known Jews—Zebulon Simentov and Ishaq Levin—remained in the country almost a decade after the Taliban took control in the mid-1990s. The reason for the animosity is not clear, but both Simentov and Levin were jailed by the Taliban after having been reported by the other. Their feud lasted until Levin's death in 2005.

From living quarters at separate ends of the same Kabul synagogue, Afghanistan's last two Jews are still feuding and still searching for their most sacred treasure—a Torah confiscated by the now ousted Taliban.

The two men glare at each other when they pass in the decaying synagogue's concrete courtyard. They planned to celebrate Passover as they do every other Jewish holiday—alone.

"I have no contact with him. He is a Muslim. He was a Taliban spy," Zebulon Simentov, 42, said of the synagogue's other inhabitant, Ishaq Levin, who doesn't know his exact age but is well into his 70s.

"When I try to speak to him he doesn't answer," says Levin. "Now he's telling everyone I changed my religion. But I am an original Jew."

Afghanistan once had a thriving Jewish community numbering some 40,000 in the late 19th century. Now, as far as anyone knows, the community consists of only Simentov and Levin—and they despise each other.

Afghanistan and eastern Persia—today's Iran—are home to a unique Torah design that uses one flat and two round finials to wrap the holy scrolls. The rest of the world's Jews use just one pair.

The Taliban confiscated the synagogue's sole remaining Torah about three years ago. Simentov has formally asked Afghanistan's post–Taliban Interior Ministry to locate and return it.

The scroll was last known to be in the hands of Khairullah Khair Khawa, a former Taliban Interior Minister who later became governor of the eastern province of Herat, said Sherjah, deputy head of the Interior Ministry's criminal investigation department who like many Afghans uses just one name.

Simentov accused Levin of wanting to sell the Torah; Levin said Simentov provoked the Taliban into taking it by telling Muslim women their fortunes and prescribing medicine and love potions for them.

The origins of their feud are murky, but both Levin and Simentov had been jailed by the Taliban after being reported by the other for alleged offenses ranging from religious harassment to running a brothel.

In his dimly lit room below the synagogue's second-floor sanctuary, Levin gets on all fours to describe the position he said the Taliban made him assume when they beat him. In the sanctuary upstairs, the paint is peeling, birds nest in cracking light fixtures and old prayer books crumble in the holy ark that used to house the Torah.

Levin said he didn't expect things to improve much under Afghanistan's new leaders.

"Under the new rules, a person who is rich is good and a person who is poor is bad," he said, adding that he'd like to join his children in Israel but doesn't have the funds to travel.

Besides, he said, he's afraid of what would happen to the synagogue if he left.

"I was alone in this place for 26 years," Levin said.

Born in Herat, the other Afghan city where Judaism once flourished, Simentov spent much of his life outside of Afghanistan but returned nearly four years ago to set up a carpet business.

He brought money donated by Afghan Jews in Israel for a guardhouse and wall around Kabul's Jewish cemetery. He executed the mission, even though all the tombstones had been destroyed by civil war. The parched land is now covered by dry weeds and rocks.

For centuries, Afghan Jews had little contact with the outside world. In the first half of the 19th century, many Persian Jews came to Afghanistan fleeing forced conversion in the eastern Iranian city of Mashhad.

By mid-20th century, about 5,000 remained, but most emigrated after Israel's creation in 1948. The 1979 Soviet invasion drove out nearly all the rest, but Levin—the synagogue's shamash, or caretaker—stayed on.

The Soviet years, the civil warfare of the early 1990s and the Taliban rule have left the community on the verge of extinction.

Still, Levin and Simentov say they have no intention of ending their feud. Each lights candles on the Sabbath, kisses the mezuzah upon entering the synagogue and avoids eating leavened bread on Passover.

With crude sticks for furniture, they sleep on floor mats and don't dare venture into the other's territory inside the synagogue grounds.

"May God help us," Levin said.

The Systemic Abuse of Women in Post-Taliban Afghanistan

Human Rights Watch

Human Rights Watch (HRW) is an international nonprofit dedicated to protecting human rights around the world. In the following viewpoint, taken from the 2012 report "I Had to Run Away": The Imprisonment of Women and Girls for "Moral Crimes" in Afghanistan, HRW brings to light systemic abuses of women and girls in Afghanistan following the 2001 defeat of the Taliban. HRW compiles the stories of young Afghan women and girls who describe being arrested and prosecuted for leaving home without the permission of their husbands or families as well as zina, alleged sexual contact between unmarried individuals, which is a crime in many majority-Muslim nations.

Case of Souriya Y.: Souriya Y. was given in *baad* [a traditional practice of resolving disputes by giving a girl to the wronged family] at age 12 to marry into a family to whom her family owed compensation because Souriya's brother had run away with one of the family's daughters. Souriya says she was beaten and abused by her new husband. When she went to her father for help, he told her she should be patient.

After nine years and three children, the first of whom was born when she was 13, Souriya claims her husband accused her of running away with an enemy of his, a man with whom her husband had a long-running dispute but whom Souriya says she had not met until the first time they appeared in court together after their arrest. She was charged with "running away" and *zina* [inappropriate sexual intimacy]. She told Human Rights Watch, "My husband made this story up to get rid of me and hurt this man. He married another woman two days after I was arrested."

Souriya was convicted and sentenced to five-and-a-half years in prison. The man with whom she was accused of running away and committing *zina* was sentenced to six-and-a-half years in prison.

Souriya told Human Rights Watch that she was pregnant when she [was] arrested and gave birth in the prison to a baby boy, who died after three weeks. On the issue of *baad*, Souriya said:

> Baad is a bad way. If [some people] fall in love, they should be allowed to marry. Why I should be the victim of them? If such a thing is happening, [at least there] should be an agreement that the girl is treated well, that my husband will love me and will treat me well. . . .

Punishing Those Who Help Women "Run Away"

Case of Parween D. and Roya S.: Parween D., 21, and Roya S., age unknown, were close friends. According to the court file, Parween and Roya spoke on the phone one day, and Roya confided that she was having serious problems with her husband, and asked if she could bring her children and come to stay with Parween and her husband. Parween, according to her statement to the police, told Roya that she was very welcome if her husband wanted to come with her or gave her permission, but she should not leave without his permission, since this would bring trouble.

Nevertheless, sometime later, Roya and her four children arrived at Parween's house. Parween and her husband realized after a day or two that Roya had, in fact, run away from her husband, and he did not know where she was. Concerned about bringing trouble on themselves, they called Roya's husband and told him that his wife and children were with them. Roya's oldest child overheard the phone call and, according to the court file, told his mother. The next morning, Roya and her youngest child had disappeared.

Roya's husband arrived to collect his other three children. He and the children travelled back to his home city with Parween and her husband. As they reached the city, Roya's husband told police at a checkpoint that Parween and her husband had helped his wife escape from him. They were both arrested, and charged under article 130 of the constitution with assisting Roya in "escaping from home."

The primary court convicted them and sentenced each to three years of imprisonment. The appeal court confirmed their conviction, but reduced each of their sentences to one year. In reaching its decision, the appeal court wrote:

> If the accused [Parween and her husband] had really had good intention they would have informed the husband of [Roya] in a way that she did not know about it so that the opportunity for her second escape would not have been created. Therefore the liability of the accused people in assisting [Roya] to escape is proved and justified and the accused are found guilty in accordance with article 130 of constitution. But since the accused people committed such action unknowingly and with goodwill the judicial board sees it necessary to modify the decision. . . .

"Running Away" from Child Marriage and Abuse

Case of Bashira S.: Bashira S., 14, told Human Rights Watch that at the age of 12 her father arranged to have her marry her uncle's son, an older boy in the household in which she had grown up: "I was not happy with this engagement and getting married to him. I was 12-years-old [when] I got married to my cousin."

Bashira was soon pregnant. But the marriage went badly. "He was fighting with me, he was beating me. He said, 'You don't love me. You didn't want to marry me.'"

In 2011 she fled to an aunt's house and stayed there for 10 days. Bashira found a phone number for the Criminal Investigations Department and called their office, saying that she fled her marital house "because of so much fighting and beating." The police put her in a shelter for 15 days, but she said that the investigators also called her in-laws, and they accused her of running away to see the son of the aunt to whom she had fled. She denied this:

> I just wanted to inform them, to get my divorce, and get released from that man. . . . I said, "No, it is not the case, I don't love him [the aunt's son] and I didn't love him. I only came here because I cannot go to any stranger, somebody whom I don't know. . . . [So] that is why I came here." But then they put me here [in a juvenile detention center].

Bashira was arrested and then convicted of "running away" and sentenced to two years in juvenile detention. Her aunt's son was not arrested. When asked what the government could do differently to help girls in her situation, she said:

> I don't know. I went to the government to ask for help and they brought me here [the juvenile rehabilitation center]. We don't have any problem here. It is better than home. We have food and clothes and medical care.

When she is released, Bashira plans to go back to the shelter.

> She [my stepmother] is the only one who comes. She says go back to your husband and live with him. I say, "No, I can't after all this." They will beat me more. I want a divorce. My husband

A woman in a burqa walks alone past buildings in Kabul destroyed by heavy shelling in 1994. Critics assert that women in Afghanistan have suffered greatly from the armed conflicts and from systemic oppression by the Taliban. © Robert Nickelsberg/Getty Image News/Getty Images.

said [in court], "I will take you home and then I will give you a divorce." I said, "No, you will kill me."

Bashira's son is with her husband. . . .

Women Are Convicted of "Sexual Immorality" After Being Kidnapped and Raped

Case of Tahmina J.: Tahmina J., 18, fled her home in 2011 to escape domestic abuse and forced marriage to a cousin. She told Human Rights Watch:

> My mother was always beating me and fighting with me. I always said to her, "I will escape from you one day." I was engaged to someone, but I loved [a male friend]. . . . My mother's brother had made the arrangement [for a marriage]. They didn't tell me.

Tahmina fled her house to go in search of the boy she liked. According to court records, Tahmina went without permission from her parents' home to the home of her aunt, who lived in the same neighborhood of the boy. She did not know where he lived, but hoped to find him. That night, she left her aunt's house without permission to go to look for him. Without finding him, she encountered two men in the street who she said abducted her by force and raped her.

In her statement to the police, Tahmina stated:

> They took me to an abandoned house. I tried to resist them doing *zina* with me, but they were two people so I couldn't and they did the bad act. They attacked my reputation and did *zina* with me. Then they handed me to the *wakili guzar* [neighborhood elder]. He took me to the police station.

According to the police report, the two men were brought to the police station in 2011. "I identified them as the two people who by force assaulted me and did *zina* with me," her statement says.

Police records noted that a medical exam of Tahmina indicated recent and past sexual activity. Many of the women and girls interviewed for this report described being subjected to gynecological examinations, and court files also indicated the routine use of and reliance upon such examinations for the purpose of determining virginity and whether a woman or girl had engaged in recent sexual intercourse. Use of such examinations was not limited to rape cases, and examinations did not focus on whether forced intercourse had taken place. Although medical examinations can be a legitimate form of investigation in a case of alleged sexual assault, gynecological examinations that purport to determine virginity have no medical accuracy. As party to the International Covenant on Civil and Political Rights, Afghanistan is obliged to protect women from cruel and inhuman treatment and discrimination, and to ensure their right to privacy. Coercive virginity tests violate all three of those obligations. Virginity tests also violate guarantees of freedom from discrimination in the Convention on the Elimination of All Forms of Discrimination against Women (CEDAW). The CEDAW Committee has stated that it views with the "gravest concern the practice of forced gynecological examinations of women . . . including of women prisoners while in custody." The committee "emphasized that such coercive practices were degrading, discriminatory and unsafe and constituted a violation by state authorities of the bodily integrity, person and dignity of women." Conducting virginity tests without the informed consent of the girl or woman violates her right to bodily integrity, dignity, privacy, and equality before the law, and would amount to a sexual assault. Such assaults cannot be justified, being based on an intrinsically discriminatory presumption that an examination of female virginity can be a legitimate interest of the state. Under international law virginity tests committed in custody constitute cruel and inhuman treatment. These exams are painful, degrading, and frightening. The file then claims that Tahmina gave conflicting accounts about her earlier sexual activity, saying initially that she had once had sex with a cousin at an earlier point, at another point saying she had had sex with her friend. There is no indication in the court file that the police inquired about whether this prior sex was consensual. In the end, the police accused her of two instances of *zina*, one with the two men she accused of raping her, and another with the friend.

A prosecutor in the case told Human Rights Watch that he was skeptical of Tahmina's allegations of rape because no witnesses had reported hearing screams when she was raped, and because of conflicts in her account relating to her earlier sexual activity. According to the prosecutor:

> She said they took her to an abandoned house and raped her. . . . What she is saying is not completely true or certain because she said she had sex with her cousin [at an earlier point] but then later denied this. There must have been consent [with the two men] because she didn't scream or say anything until she was handed to the *wakili guzar* [neighborhood elder].

When asked whether they had investigated the allegations of forced marriage Tahmina made against her mother, the prosecutor said there were "contradictions" in her statement, including that "she had *zina* with her cousin but later said it was with someone else."

The court, in considering Tahmina's case, wrote, "A woman going out, especially at night, is followed by certain dangers." The court described the two men as having "sexually assaulted" Tahmina, but then notes that she had "gone with these men of her own intention and she didn't make any screaming." The court found Tahmina guilty of two counts of *zina* (once with the two men and once previously with the man she liked) plus "running away."

She was sentenced to one-and-a-half-years for having sex with her friend, two-and-a-half years for the incident with the two men in the abandoned building, and one year for "running away" from home, for a total of five years. The sentence was then reduced by half because of her status as a juvenile under Afghan law.

Date Rape Leads to Accusation of *Zina*

Case of Malalai H.: Malalai H., 18, told Human Rights Watch that one day she received a love letter from a neighbor named Ahmed. He soon sent more. Later he sent Malalai a cell phone and started calling her. "One day he came to my school and introduced himself and I saw that he was handsome," she said. "We started a relationship and saw each other all the time."

Malalai said that at one point in 2011, Ahmed traveled out of town for work for several months, and when he returned, Malalai invited him to her house when she was home alone. It proved to be a mistake. "He wanted to have sex with me. I refused. He did sex with me from the backside by force." Malalai said she thought her family "will kill me if they know," and fled her home.

I ran away because my family is very serious and I knew they would kill me so I thought it is better to commit suicide. I tried to die by jumping in front of a car but the car stopped.

Malalai said she called a friend named Sidiq for advice. He told her she should go home. She went home, but her parents had reported her missing and took her to the police and accused her of "running away" with Sidiq. Malalai and Sidiq were both arrested. Malalai says no one believes that Sidiq is entirely innocent and that she was raped by Ahmed.

When Human Rights Watch interviewed Malalai, she and Sidiq had been imprisoned for several months but had not yet had a trial. She hopes the court will find them not guilty. She has not heard from Ahmed since the rape and she does not know where he is, but she still hopes to marry him: "I have to marry Ahmed or go and die, because my life is damaged. I still love him. He said I will marry you." . . .

Women Are Imprisoned After Being Forced into Prostitution

Case of Amina R.: Amina R., 17, told Human Rights Watch that she was scheduled to be married to a man she did not want to marry. She was also unhappy at home because her mother was beating her, including in front of her future in-laws. She fled in 2011 with the help of an aunt. "My aunt gave me a phone number," she said. "She told me to call and escape with that man [whose phone number it was] and marry him instead."

Amina did as her aunt told her, only to discover that the man she had escaped with, though she was told he was not married, lived with his wife and did not actually want to marry Amina. Instead he kept her in his house, with his wife, for six months, using her as a concubine and forcing her into prostitution. She told Human Rights Watch:

> We were not married, and we did *zina*. I had sex with him and with other men. . . . First they gave me alcohol and made me unconscious, then they did this [sex] to me.

After six months, Amina said, the man "sold" her to another man. The second man wanted to take her to another city but they were stopped at a police checkpoint. The police realized that they were not married and arrested them in 2011.

When Human Rights Watch interviewed Amina she had been in detention for several months, but there had not yet been a decision in her case. She said she believed that her father plans to kill her when she is released.

Organizations to Contact

The editors have compiled the following list of organizations concerned with the issues debated in this book. The descriptions are derived from materials provided by the organizations. All have publications or information available for interested readers. The list was compiled on the date of publication of the present volume; the information provided here may change. Be aware that many organizations take several weeks or longer to respond to inquiries, so allow as much time as possible.

Afghanistan Justice Project
e-mail: info@afghanistanjusticeproject.org
website: www.afghanistanjusticeproject.org

The Afghanistan Justice Project is an independent, non-partisan, non-governmental research and advocacy organization. Since 2001 it has investigated and documented war crimes and crimes against humanity committed in Afghanistan during the Soviet occupation and Taliban era. Its website offers articles on conditions for civilians in Afghanistan and human rights abuses, including the 2005 report "Casting Shadows: War Crimes and Crimes Against Humanity, 1978–2001."

Amnesty International
5 Penn Plaza, 14th Floor
New York, NY, 10001
(212) 807-8400 • fax: (212) 463-9193
e-mail: aimember@aiusa.org
website: www.amnestyusa.org

Amnesty International is a worldwide campaign for internationally recognized human rights. Its vision is of a world in which every person enjoys all of the human rights enshrined in the Universal Declaration of Human Rights and other international human rights agreements. Its website includes various articles on Afghanistan, its annual report on human rights conditions in Afghanistan, and the report "Women in Afghanistan: A Human Rights Catastrophe."

Human Rights Watch (HRW)
350 Fifth Ave., 34th Floor
New York, NY 10118-3299
(212) 290-4700 • fax: (212) 736-1300
e-mail: hrwnyc@hrw.org
website: www.hrw.org

Founded in 1978, this non-governmental organization conducts systematic investigations of human rights abuses around the world and advocates for human dignity. HRW publishes various books and reports on specific countries—including Afghanistan. Its website includes numerous discussions of human rights and international justice issues.

**Montreal Institute for Genocide and Human Rights
Studies (MIGS)**
Concordia University
1455 De Maisonneuve Blvd.
West Montreal, Quebec, H3G 1M8 Canada
(514) 848-2424 ext. 5729 or 2404 • fax: (514) 848-4538
website: http://migs.concordia.ca

MIGS, founded in 1986, monitors native language media for early warning signs of genocide in countries deemed to be at risk of mass atrocities. The institute houses the Will to Intervene (W2I) Project, a research initiative focused on the prevention of genocide and other mass atrocities. The institute also collects and disseminates research on the historical origins of mass killings on its website. The website provides numerous links to resources focused on genocide and related issues as well as specialized sites organized by nation, region, or case.

Physicians for Human Rights (PHR)
2 Arrow Street, Suite 301
Cambridge, MA 02138
(617) 301-4200 • fax: (617) 301-4250
website: http://physiciansforhumanrights.org

Physicians for Human Rights is an independent, nonprofit organization that uses medical and scientific expertise to investigate human rights violations and advocate for justice. The organization's work in Afghanistan includes a three-year project, begun in 2009, to help the Afghan government develop processes for investigating mass graves and confronting the nation's history of unpunished war crimes. PHR also continues to investigate the alleged 2002 massacre of two thousand Taliban prisoners. Its website includes resources on war crimes and transitional justice in Afghanistan, including the report "Truth Seeking and the Role of Forensic Science."

Revolutionary Association of the Women of Afghanistan (RAWA)
PO Box 374
Quetta, Pakistan
0092-300-5541258
e-mail: rawa@rawa.org
website: www.rawa.org

RAWA was founded in 1977 to address the plight of women in Afghanistan. Since the Soviet occupation, RAWA has tirelessly advocated for secular democracy and women's rights in Afghanistan. RAWA is the oldest and most established organization of Afghan women working for women's fundamental rights in Afghanistan. The RAWA website offers numerous reports, statements, and press releases on Afghan women's rights.

STAND/United to End Genocide
1025 Connecticut Ave., Suite 310

Washington, DC 20036
(202) 556-2100
e-mail: info@standnow.org
website: www.standnow.org

STAND is the student-led division of United to End Genocide. STAND envisions a world in which the global community is willing and able to protect civilians from genocide and mass atrocities. In order to empower individuals and communities with the tools to prevent and stop genocide, STAND recommends activities such as engaging government representatives and hosting fundraisers. The organization has more than one thousand student chapters at colleges and high schools. STAND maintains numerous online resources and also provides plans for promoting action and education.

United Human Rights Council (UHRC)
104 N. Belmont Street, Suite 313
Glendale, CA 91206
(818) 507-1933
website: www.unitedhumanrights.org

The United Human Rights Council is a committee of the Armenian Youth Federation. By means of action on a grassroots level, the UHRC works toward exposing and correcting human rights violations by governments worldwide. The UHRC campaigns against violators in an effort to generate awareness through boycotts, community outreach, and education. The UHRC website focuses on the genocides of the twentieth century.

United Nations Assistance Mission in Afghanistan (UNAMA)
405 E. 42nd Street
New York, NY 10017
(212) 963-2668 ext. 6153
e-mail: spokesman-unama@un.org
website: www.unama.unmissions.org

Established in 2002 at the behest of the Afghan government, UNAMA is a political mission of the United Nations. UNAMA is focused on sustainable peace, development, and humanitarian affairs and promotes human rights and humanitarian relief in Afghanistan. Its website is a clearinghouse for up-to-date information on political developments in Afghanistan. The Key Documents and Reports section of the website offers a variety of reports on living conditions, women's rights, and the plight of civilians living in Afghanistan. The Publications section of the website includes current and back issues of its newspaper *Afghanistan and the United Nations* and quarterly magazine *Afghan Update.*

List of Primary Source Documents

The editors have compiled the following list of documents that either broadly address genocide and persecution or more narrowly focus on the topic of this volume. The full text of these documents is available from multiple sources in print and online.

Convention Against Torture and Other Cruel, Inhuman, or Degrading Treatment or Punishment, United Nations, 1974

This draft resolution adopted by the United Nations General Assembly in 1974 opposes any nation's use of torture, unusually harsh punishment, and unfair imprisonment.

Convention on the Prevention and Punishment of the Crime of Genocide, United Nations, December 9, 1948

This resolution of the United Nations General Assembly defines genocide in legal terms and advises participating countries to prevent and punish actions of genocide in war and peacetime.

Principles of International Law Recognized in the Charter of the Nuremberg Tribunal, United Nations International Law Commission, 1950

After World War II (1939–1945) the victorious allies legally tried surviving leaders of Nazi Germany in the German city of Nuremberg. The proceedings established standards for international law that were affirmed by the United Nations and by later court tests. Among other standards, national leaders can be held responsible for crimes against humanity, which might include "murder, extermination, deportation, enslavement, and other inhuman acts."

Rome Statute of the International Criminal Court, July 17, 1998

This treaty established the International Criminal Court. It creates the court's functions, jurisdiction, and structure.

State of the Union Address, US President Jimmy Carter, January 23, 1980

Given just one month after Soviet troops entered Afghanistan, President Carter's 1980 State of the Union Address made clear that Soviet action in Afghanistan, and the larger perception of aggressive expansion by the USSR, was seen as a threat to peace throughout the globe.

United Nations General Assembly Resolution 36/34 on "The Situation in Afghanistan and Its Implications for International Peace and Security," United Nations, November 18, 1981

This resolution is the first time the United Nations General Assembly acknowledged the growing refugee and humanitarian crisis in Afghanistan under Soviet occupation. The UN would go on to affirm this same resolution, almost verbatim, for the next decade (throughout the entire Soviet occupation of Afghanistan).

United Nations General Assembly Resolution 96 on the Crime of Genocide, United Nations, December 11, 1946

This resolution of the United Nations General Assembly affirms that genocide is a crime under international law.

Universal Declaration of Human Rights, United Nations, 1948

Soon after its founding, the United Nations approved this general statement of individual rights it hoped would apply to citizens of all nations.

Whitaker Report on Genocide, United Nations, 1985

This report addresses the question of the prevention and punishment of the crime of genocide. It calls for the establishment of an international criminal court and a system of universal jurisdiction to ensure that genocide is punished.

For Further Research

Books

Raja Anwar and Fred Halliday, *The Tragedy of Afghanistan: A First-Hand Account*. New York: Verso, 1990.

Gennady Bocharov, *Russian Roulette: Afghanistan Through Russian Eyes*. New York: HarperCollins, 1990.

Arthur Bonner, *Among the Afghans*. Durham, NC: Duke University Press, 1988.

Gerard Chaliand, *Report from Afghanistan*. New York: Penguin, 1982.

Melody Ermachild Chavis, *Meena, Heroine of Afghanistan: The Martyr Who Founded RAWA, the Revolutionary Association of the Women of Afghanistan.* New York: St. Martin's Griffin, 2004.

Steve Coll, *Ghost Wars: The Secret History of the CIA, Afghanistan, and Bin Laden, from the Soviet Invasion to September 10, 2001*. New York: Penguin, 2004.

Gilles Dorronsoro, *Revolution Unending: Afghanistan, 1979 to the Present*. New York: Columbia University Press, 2005.

Martin Ewans, *Afghanistan: A Short History of Its People and Politics*. New York: Harper Perennial, 2002.

Kathy Gannon, *I Is for Infidel: From Holy War to Holy Terror in Afghanistan*. New York: PublicAffairs, 2006.

Edward Girardet, *Afghanistan: The Soviet War*. New York: Routledge, 2011.

Edward Girardet, *Killing the Cranes: A Reporter's Journey Through Three Decades of War in Afghanistan*. White River Junction, VT: Chelsea Green, 2011.

Larry P. Goodson, *Afghanistan's Endless War: State Failure, Regional Politics, and the Rise of the Taliban.* Seattle: University of Washington Press, 2001.

Michael Griffin, *Reaping the Whirlwind: The Taliban Movement in Afghanistan.* London: Pluto, 2001.

Emmanuel Guibert, *The Photographer: Into War-Torn Afghanistan with Doctors Without Borders.* New York: First Second, 2009.

Roy Gutman, *How We Missed the Story: Osama Bin Laden, the Taliban and the Hijacking of Afghanistan.* Washington, DC: United States Institute of Peace Press, 2008.

M. Hassan Kakar, *Afghanistan: The Soviet Invasion and the Afghan Response, 1979–1982.* Berkeley: University of California Press, 1995.

Rosanne Klass, *Afghanistan: The Great Game Revisited.* Lanham, MD: University Press of America, 1990.

Douglas J. Maceachin, *Predicting the Soviet Invasion of Afghanistan: The Intelligence Community's Record.* Darby, PA: Diane Publishing Company, 2003.

Peter Tomsen, *The Wars of Afghanistan: Messianic Terrorism, Tribal Conflicts, and the Failures of Great Powers.* New York: PublicAffairs, 2011.

Marvin G. Weinbaum, *Pakistan and Afghanistan: Resistance and Reconstruction.* Boulder, CO: Westview Press, 1994.

Periodicals and Internet Sources

The Afghanistan Justice Project, "Casting Shadows: War Crimes and Crimes Against Humanity: 1978–2001," Open Society Institute, 2005. www.unhcr.org.

Amnesty International, "Afghanistan: Public Executions and Amputations on Increase," Amnesty International in Asia and the Pacific, May 1998. www.amnesty.org.

Steve Coll, "Spies, Lies and the Distortion of History," *Washington Post*, February 24, 2002.

Dinesh D'Souza, "President Ronald Reagan: Winning the Cold War," *American History*, October 2003. www.historynet.com.

Carlotta Gall, "In Afghanistan, Where Pregnancy Is Still a Minefield," *New York Times*, June 23, 2002. www.nytimes.com.

Carlotta Gall and Judith Miller, "Women Suffer Most in Afghan Health Crisis, Experts Say," *New York Times*, October 27, 2003. www.nytimes.com.

Kathy Gannon, "Afghanistan Unbound," *Foreign Affairs*, vol. 38, no. 3, 2004.

Harry Gelman, "The Politburo's Management of Its America Problem," Rand Corporation, April 1981. www.rand.org.

Virginia Heffernan, "The Feminist Hawks," *New York Times Magazine*, August 23, 2009.

Human Rights Watch, "We Want to Live as Humans: Repression of Women and Girls in Western Afghanistan," Human Rights Watch, December 17, 2002. www.hrw.org.

Vincent Iacopino and Zohra Rasekh et al., "The Taliban's War on Women: A Health and Human Rights Crisis in Afghanistan," Physicians for Human Rights, 1998. http://physiciansforhumanrights.org.

Sidney Jones et al., "Afghanistan," *Human Rights Watch World Report 1989*, January 2, 1990. www.hrw.org.

Artemy Kalinovsky, "The Blind Leading the Blind: Soviet Advisors, Counter-Insurgency and Nation-Building in Afghanistan," *Cold War International History Project Working Paper*, Woodrow Wilson International Center for Scholars, January 2010. http://wilsoncenter.org.

Michael T. Kaufman, "Afghan Driver Says He Saw Soldiers Blind and Strangle Children," *New York Times*, September 11, 1979.

Rosanne Klass, "Lifting the Curtain on Afghanistan's Horror," *Wall Street Journal*, January 24, 1983.

Fariba Nawa, "Afghanistan, Inc.," *CorpWatch*, May 2, 2006. www.corpwatch.org.

Rachel Reid, "The 'Ten-Dollar Talib' and Women's Rights," Human Rights Watch, July 13 2010. www.hrw.org.

Carol J. Riphenburg, "Post-Taliban Afghanistan: Changed Outlook for Women?," *Asian Survey*, 2004.

Russian International News Agency, "Retired General Says Soviet Incursion of Afghanistan Justified," *RIA Novosti*, December 27, 2012. http://en.rian.ru.

Sharifullah Sahak, "In Bold Display, Taliban Order Stoning Deaths," *New York Times*, August 16, 2010. www.nytimes.com.

Rob Schultheis, "The Soviets' Ugly Exit," *Washington Post*, January 8, 1989.

Ken Silverstein, "Six Questions for Patricia Gossman on Afghanistan," *Harper's Magazine*, April 28, 2001. harpers.org.

Richard Stengel, "The Plight of Afghan Women: A Disturbing Picture," Time.com, July 29, 2010. www.time.com.

United Nations Assistance Mission in Afghanistan and the Office of the High Commissioner for Human Rights, "A Long Way to Go: Implementation of the Elimination of Violence Against Women Law in Afghanistan," November 2011. www.ohchr.org.

Websites

Cold War International History Project of the Woodrow Wilson Center Digital Archive (www.wilsoncenter.org

/digital-archive). Subsections of this site focused on Afghanistan and the Soviet invasion include a varied collection of primary documents on this period of Afghan history, stretching from 1968 to 2004.

Physicians for Human Rights (http://physiciansforhuman rights.org). Founded in 1986 by a small group of doctors seeking to harness the expertise and authority of physicians in investigating human rights abuses, Physicians for Human Rights has since completed investigations in more than forty countries. The Afghanistan section of its website includes articles on the group's work in Afghanistan, including investigating mass atrocities and developing methods for international forensic investigations.

United Nations News Centre (www.un.org/News). The United Nations News Centre archives articles from the UN News Service that report on humanitarian crises and violent conflict worldwide. The News Focus: Afghanistan section of the site collects all of the UN's resources concerning ongoing international activity and conflicts in Afghanistan.

Index